RETIREMENT
MONEY
SECRETS

A Financial Insider's Guide
to Income Independence

STEVE SELENGUT

Retirement Money Secrets is dedicated to the hundreds of clients I have worked with throughout my management career. It should allow all of you to pass on your income success stories to your heirs.

CONTENTS

PART II: 6 STEPS TO MORE RETIREMENT MONEY 4I

INTRODUCTION

I F YOU'VE OPENED this book, you're probably trying to figure out how to invest your money so you'll have a secure retirement. You might be at or near retirement age, still in your 40s, or looking to join the FIRE (Financial Independence, Retire Early) movement.

Well, you're in the right place. Since 1979, I've been helping people prepare for and live well in retirement. With this book, I'm putting my whole investing system into your hands, showing you step-by-step how to generate all the income you'll need when you retire—and beyond.

Not ready for retirement? The approach you discover in these pages will enable you to achieve your desired retirement income sooner and more safely with your rollover 401(k) account or IRA, regardless of market conditions.

Want to retire early? This book can help you do that, too.

WHO I AM, AND WHY MY INVESTING ADVICE IS DIFFERENT

If you're wondering where my advice comes from, I've been investing money for more than 50 years. After seeing strong success in my own small portfolio in my 20s, I became an SEC-registered professional investment manager in 1979.

In 44 years as a pro, I've personally managed hundreds of individual portfolios. When I sold my practice in 2023, I had over $110 million in capital under management in nearly 300 separate client accounts, and the two clients who started with me in 1979 were still on board.

Now, in semi-retirement, I live an unrestricted lifestyle funded by the income from my own portfolios. I've always invested my own funds using the same methodology I developed for my clients. In recent years, I've traveled extensively without having to sell a single stock or fund to get the money for a trip.

WHY I WROTE THIS BOOK

I was driven to create this book because it makes me heartsick to watch people starve in retirement. And yet, that's what millions of people worldwide end up doing.

Most don't understand how to develop a dependable, growing stream of investment income so they can retire worry-free. If the stock market tanks, they're up nights worried about their nest egg.

Meeting one-on-one or in small groups with frustrated investors and talking them through my investing approach can't get this information out there fast enough. So, I've put my entire system into this book, hoping it can help many more people achieve financial independence.

I want to show you how to create an ample, growing retirement fund—one that generates income you can rely on, no matter which way the stock market or interest rates are moving,

Interested? Then read on.

WHAT YOU'LL LEARN

I'm going to introduce you to a simple, six-step method of investing safely to maximize your retirement income. Some of the concepts I'll talk about will be familiar to you, but some are likely to be either new or totally different.

The most important thing as you make your way through this book is to keep an open mind. Don't worry—we're going to take it slow. I'll explain everything in plain English. There are plenty of examples that help illustrate the concepts, too.

Because I've been investing peoples' money for years, I tend to talk in investor lingo. To make sure I keep it simple and clear, this book recreates a conversation I had with a retired couple I met on a cruise not long ago.

They were curious to learn how my retirement investing approach reliably generates more money than the norm, and they asked a lot of questions.

They didn't know anything about my investing philosophy when we first sat down, so my hope is that they will prove to be a good stand-in for you. I think they asked all the questions you'll have. There's also a Q&A at the end of the book with my Facebook investor group members that provides even more answers.

One style note: Since this entire book is me talking to these prospects, explaining things and answering questions, there are no quotes around what I say. They only appear with what others are saying. That way, your eyes won't cross from all the quote marks!

NOT AN ACCOUNTANT OR ATTORNEY

Please keep in mind throughout the book that I'm not an accountant or attorney. No information, ideas, suggestions, or thoughts expressed in this book should be interpreted as either legal or tax advice. Laws and the tax code change constantly and vary from state to state, so be sure to consult your local tax or legal professional before taking any investment actions.

This book is also not intended to offer investment advice. The examples used here should not be considered specific buy, sell, or hold recommendations. They're intended to illustrate how my principles work to generate high income.

Remember that markets change over time, and examples in the book are from the past.

BE AN INFORMED INVESTOR

By the end of this book, you'll understand enough about income-focused investing to manage your portfolio yourself. But if you don't want to be bothered, you could also hire an investment manager to do it for you. You'll be able to ask all the right questions to make sure your managers do a good job and really earn their fees.

Finally, you could take a hybrid approach. Many investors who use my approach do most of their portfolio management themselves but get a bit of consulting from me. At the end of this book, I'll tell you more about how you can do that. I'll also list some free resources to help you on your journey.

Ready to learn a low-risk approach that will result in your investments earning more money and help you enjoy a carefree retirement? Let's get started.

PART 1

The Trouble With
Traditional Investing

ONE: I Meet a Curious Couple

WHEREVER I GO in the world, I end up talking to people about how they're investing for retirement. It's my passion and my business—and Americans *love* to talk about money.

The May 2023 evening that my wife Sandie and I landed in Amsterdam was no exception. We had just checked into our hotel in the city center, which was our launching point for a three-country river cruise. After finding our light-filled room and receiving our suitcases from the bellhop, we changed into the casual wear we'd brought for Europe's spring weather, which is cooler than our home of Charleston, South Carolina. Sandie ran a brush through her curly reddish-blonde hair, applied a quick touch of lipstick, and we headed back out.

We strolled toward the hotel restaurant for a planned meet-and-greet meal with our fellow travelers. We were excited to be here for a few days before boarding the Viking riverboat headed through Germany, France, and Switzerland.

Sandie and I have been best friends since we first met at 12 years old and quickly became inseparable. This was already shaping up to be another memorable journey in our lifetime of adventures together. Besides our love for each other, we share a love of discovering and learning about different cultures.

We walked across the hotel courtyard to the complex's outdoor, European-fusion restaurant, sinking into comfortable, sherbet-colored chairs at a large table our tour host had reserved for all its passengers. There was so much to take in, it was hard to concentrate on the menu.

Sounds drifted in from behind us … the clink of glasses in the bar, the burble of the courtyard fountain. With them came scents emanating from the kitchen: frying schnitzel, garlic and oregano in pasta, burgers grilling. The city's main canal, Herengracht, was filled with watercraft of all descriptions—fancy houseboats, decrepit tiny schooners, and everything in between.

The road alongside was jammed with strolling shoppers, cabs, and bicyclists ringing their bells. The beauty of the buildings on the canal immediately brought smiles to our faces.

The sun began to set, turning the clouds to gold. As we soaked up the atmosphere and contemplated what to order, we were joined by another couple who caught our attention right away. Like us, they were in their 70s. John Crane is tall, with wire-rimmed glasses and a look that reminds Sandie of the movie director Sydney Pollack. His wife, Jean, is even taller, with natural gray hair and a gentle, soft-spoken demeanor.

The Cranes introduced themselves, and we soon felt like old friends as we discovered that we shared the same passion for foreign travel. It was a perfect start to our trip. We relaxed on the patio, picked at our salads and—with our thirst addressed by Heineken and local wine— settled in to learn about each other's lives.

WORKING AND SAVING

John's career was straightforward, we learned. He was an IBM engineer when he retired, with a few years at other tech companies along the way. That made sense to me, since he seemed to be a logical, just-the-facts kind of guy. In my experience, engineers are generally resistant to change, so I made a mental note of it.

Since leaving IBM, John kept busy serving as a volunteer usher at his state's legislature. This was in line with my impression of the Cranes as fit, healthy, active semi-retirees.

It turned out Jean was a lifelong teacher, now retired. My wife filled the Cranes in on her own varied career as a paralegal, commercial artist who'd painted murals in restaurants, and, finally, compliance officer for my investment-management firm. Sandie also plays in a ladies golf group and is a proud South Carolina turtle patrol participant. Jean shared that she volunteers as a homework tutor at her local library and is an avid knitter.

Another thing we had in common was grown-up children we were proud of and grandkids we adored. In our case, both our children were pursuing careers where they could make a difference: Our daughter worked for a nonprofit that helped the homeless before transitioning to a job in solar energy, while our son is a marine biologist for the state of Virginia. Our granddaughter was at Wofford College in Spartanburg, South Carolina, majoring in Spanish and looking toward a law career, possibly overseas, while her cousin had a solid job in IT.

The Cranes outpaced us in this department, with three accomplished, grown children and more grandkids than we could brag about.

MY INVESTING ORIGIN STORY

After scanning our phones to share photos of our kids and grandkids, John asked me what I do that requires a compliance officer. From that point, the money conversation was inevitable.

After graduating from Gettysburg College in Pennsylvania, I began my business career at a major financial services firm. The rule, I told them, was you had to work there 12 years to fully vest in their pension plan, so I planned to stay that long. After seven years in administration, helping to develop an industry-first computerized policy records program, I switched to the pension and investment department, and secured an MBA in professional management from Pace University

Something else happened during those early career days, too. When I was in my teens, I gave my dad all the money I'd saved from doing odd jobs and asked him to invest it for me. My dad handed the task over to his attorney. Apparently, the attorney did well with it, as by 1970, my portfolio was worth $70,000—a decent chunk of change in those days.

The year I turned 25, I told them, my dad decided to hand portfolio management over to me. My initial goal was just to never lose any of it.

That got a chuckle from the Cranes.

As it turned out, I would well exceed that modest goal. This portfolio was my opportunity to study stock movements and learn how markets operated. From early on, I gravitated toward dividend stocks.

Eventually, I found a woman broker—rare back then—to advise me and help me find more winning stocks. With a little help from her, I began trading various companies' stocks (aka equities) more actively, cashing out some stocks when they went higher and reinvesting in ones I thought were undervalued. The result was a well-diversified portfolio of equities, with a few tax-exempt municipal bonds and corporate bond unit trusts.

Meanwhile, things were falling apart at my job. I felt my company was engaged in unethical dealings in their defined-contribution division. I ended up being a whistleblower long before it became fashionable. It was before there were any legal protections, so I knew I'd be fired for speaking up.

Before departing, I fired off a letter to the company's board members and to all the customers I worked with, telling them what was going on. The good news was that I'd been carefully laying the groundwork for my next career.

When I left that job in '79, the portfolio was worth $500,000. We had just bought a new house, and even with that expense, we were able to live off my portfolio income.

The Cranes' jaws dropped in unison. I related how I built a business around my own investing success, looking for people who'd let me manage their money, too. My two original clients, a dentist and a restaurateur, are still clients today.

"Wow," John said. "You've been investing for a long time, and your results sound impressive."

Jean nodded in agreement. "Are you with an investment firm that we'd know?" he asked.

Nope, I replied. Been an independent, private portfolio manager for a long time now.

"I'd love to have you have a look at our portfolio sometime and give me a tip or two, if it's not rude to ask," John added. "I imagine you probably get asked a lot."

I smiled. Not at all—happy to do that when we get back home, I said. But before we get into the details of how you're investing for retirement, let me ask you something: What are your goals for your portfolio? What do you hope to achieve with your investments?

John didn't have to think long. "Well, to be able to do what you do," he said. "Live off income from our portfolio."

I nodded. I think that should be the goal of all retirement portfolios, I told him. But the way most Americans invest, it doesn't work out that way. Am I right?

Jean smiled sadly. "Yes," she said. "The income from our retirement accounts falls far short of the withdrawals we want to make all too often."

It turned out the Cranes had one other retirement goal on their list. "I've also been trying to save to get a vacation place in Maine," John added. "I have my eye on this sweet property on the water. I'm thinking that as we get a bit older, we'll want to spend more and more time there. I love that part of the Northeast coast."

This was interesting, since it would require quite a lot of additional cash beyond their regular monthly expenses. Is your portfolio growing in value, or creating enough income where you think you can make it happen? I asked.

He sighed. "Not so far," he said.

WHEN RETIREMENT INVESTING FALLS SHORT

Having had my suspicions confirmed about the Cranes' investments, I asked one more question, though I suspected I already knew the answer.

If your portfolio isn't generating enough income to pay for all your expenses, and you're basically retired now, I said, then how did you pay for this trip? I mean, if that's something you're willing to share.

John looked down and studied his half-eaten plate of schnitzel for a few moments before he answered.

"I cashed in a lot of shares in one of my mutual funds to get the money for this trip," he said. "Not the first time we've done that, either."

I checked out his body language—the slumped shoulders and downcast eyes. I'm going to guess you're not totally comfortable with having to sell part of your assets to afford your trips, I said. In the investing business, we call that "invading principal to pay the bills."

Another way to think about your principal is as working capital, I added. Your money may be tied up in stocks or bonds, but this is the money you have for investing, that you can put to work generating income. Ideally, you never want working capital to shrink. Am I right?

He nodded his agreement. Jean looked like she felt even more uncomfortable than John did with the idea that they were slowly consuming their retirement assets.

When someone tells me that they have to sell assets to afford their lifestyle, I always feel frustrated. That's not how retirement investing is supposed to work. A successful investment plan should generate enough money to provide for your needs, not assets you regularly have to sell to pay your bills.

Also, liquidating your retirement assets creates a downward spiral that leads to a diminished lifestyle. It means your portfolio will likely generate even less income in the future. But I know this is how many retirees manage their finances.

I thought about how to respond to this news. I didn't want to make my new friends feel bad, so rather than grilling them about how their retirement accounts were performing or criticizing his investing approach right off, I gave them a quick, big picture look at how we fund our own travels.

Since you know we live off portfolio income, I told the Cranes, you probably won't be surprised to hear that we didn't cash in any assets to pay for this trip. It's paid for out of our portfolio income. Our required minimum distributions (RMDs) are more than covered by IRA income, so our pool of working capital is still growing. Our joint portfolio pays for all our expenses, every month, and still has income left over to reinvest.

The couple took that in. "That sounds like a dream come true," John said. "How do you manage that?"

Happy to tell you, but it's kind of a long story, I said. First, why don't you give me a general sense of how you're investing your money now? That'll show me what you already know, so I don't bore you with the basics. Then, I can explain what I do differently.

"Sure thing," he said.

TWO: Investing the Old-Fashioned Way

A S THE CRANES described their retirement savings, we ordered another round of drinks, the ladies opting for white wine while I switched to single-malt Scotch and John sampled a Grolsch.

For starters, the couple both received monthly Social Security checks. Jean also had a state pension from her career teaching public school.

Her pension was a typical defined-benefit plan, meaning that it provides a guaranteed monthly income that grants her some financial security. As with annuities and Social Security, you get back money that's been set aside for you over the years, plus a portion of the income produced by the fund. Pension plan investment rules are extremely strict, so they're quite safe for producing dependable income. John had a pension from IBM, which functioned much like Jean's pension.

The sexier part of his retirement holdings, in his view, was that he'd earned 4,000 shares of IBM stock in his years at Big Blue. It was clear those shares—and their 4 percent dividends—were his favorite holding.

"My investing began with IBM stock options," he explained. "I love getting those dividend checks."

When I wondered aloud what percent of his portfolio the IBM stock made up, he guesstimated about 7 percent of the total.

For now, I kept to myself the knowledge that this meant the Cranes were overexposed in this stock. Though it's a super blue-chip stock that was part of my original 1970 portfolio, that still puts them at risk, if IBM hit hard times and saw its stock price sink—or worse, decided to cut back its dividends. IBM did fall below the S&P investment-grade rating at least once in the past.

John also owned other stocks he'd taken a liking to over the years, purchased with inherited family money. These holdings, some ETFs and mutual funds were in a joint trust account. John also had a significant rollover IRA portfolio funded from a variety of 401(k)s he'd started with previous employers. The primary advantages of these retirement accounts are that contributions are tax deductible and any dividends or growth in the portfolio's value is tax-deferred until funds are withdrawn in retirement.

None of the other trust account securities paid much in dividends. But the portfolio itself was certainly large enough, I thought, to eventually help purchase that Maine property John wanted—if it were better invested.

All these retirement plans—401(k)s included—are known as defined-contribution plans since you deposit a set amount of your paycheck into the account monthly. Many employers match employee contributions by as much as 50 percent, a benefit that shouldn't be ignored. Unlike pensions, there's no guaranteed benefit—it depends on how well your investment choices perform over time.

TAKING YOUR EYE OFF THE BALL

I needed to tease out a bit more information to give the Cranes any advice.

Besides the individual equities, how is your IRA money invested? I asked. Are you in mutual funds, government, or corporate bond funds? Any funds added since the 401(k) rollover?

"Honestly, I can barely remember," he said. "I haven't reviewed the mix in a while. I think they're mostly in a few different mutual funds, just based on the names of them. I know some are from Black-Rock, some are Vanguard, and all the dividends are reinvested automatically."

I asked John to take a guess at how diversified the portfolio was. How much of his retirement money was spread between these stock funds and individual equities like his IBM stock? How much was in income-producing securities such as bonds, mortgages, or real estate funds, such as REITs (real estate investment trusts)?

"I think it's nearly all in stocks," he said. I bit my tongue, wanting to point out that at his age, it'd be smarter to rely more on securities designed to produce dependable income. It was hard to stay in information-gathering mode, but I didn't want to shut him down with too much negative critique until he'd told his whole story.

It sounded like none of the Cranes' portfolios were particularly well diversified. I would be surprised if the whole portfolio produced 3 percent in spending money, much less than most retirees need. On the plus side, there were probably plenty of securities they could sell at a profit now, and hundreds of excellent new income opportunities they could select.

WAITING OUT THE DOWNTURNS

There was one more issue I wanted to feel the Cranes out on before I talked to them about the pitfalls of their investing approach.

I bet you felt flush back in 2019, with the market on such a long upswing, I said. They nodded in agreement.

But how have you been feeling since last year, with the big correction in the markets? I asked.

Their faces changed immediately, showing dismay. Jean rolled her eyes and practically shuddered.

"It's awful!" she said. "We're basically stuck holding our mutual funds and individual stocks while their value keeps going down, down, down. It's still not clear how long we'll have to wait for the market to recover. We've had to tighten our belts for a while and tough it out and sell at a loss to do things like this trip."

Here's a crazy question, I said to them. What if you didn't have to worry about market cycles, the ups and downs, affecting your portfolio's value anymore?

They looked at me like I was insane.

What if instead, I continued, you invested using a strategy where your retirement income would remain high, whether the market went up or down—or, for that matter, whether interest rates were high or low? And you can take advantage of the downturns.

John pushed his plate aside and scooted forward in his chair. "I'm all ears," he said.

THREE: Why Traditional Investing Focuses on the Wrong Goals

A S I FINISHED my Scotch, I took a minute to think about the best way to introduce the Cranes to a different way of investing. I decided that first they needed to know the pitfalls of their current investing approach—that is, the way most Americans invest for retirement.

I'm happy to share the system I use that produces reliable income, no matter what the market is doing, I said. But first, I think it's important to understand *why* your retirement accounts aren't making the money you need. The whole mainstream approach to investing for retirement that you've used all your life has some fundamental flaws. And it all starts with how many people begin investing in their company 401(k).

The Cranes looked at each other, a bit confused, while Sandie busied herself nibbling at her meal. She'd heard this story before.

THE DOWNSIDE OF BUY-AND-HOLD

Think about the basic premise most investors use, I said. The idea is that you own a mix of various ETFs, mutual funds, stocks and bonds, all of high quality and in various sectors and styles. And that allows you to participate in the steady growth of market values over time. Is that about right?

They nodded. "We know diversification is important," said John, "though, now that you made me think about it, I guess over time maybe we haven't been as diversified as we should be. Our market values have certainly grown over the years, though."

I picked up the thread: But the increase in value didn't create a dependable cash flow that would pay all your bills in retirement. Right?

They looked at each other and seemed to give it a minute of thought. Finally, Jean answered. "Yes, it is. So for now, we just hang onto those mutual funds and wait for them to go up in value over time," she said.

I lit up. That's right, I said. It's called "buy-and-hold" investing. Also known as "set it and forget it."

The buy-and-hold approach focuses on market value growth, instead of income production, I explained. You hope that the market value of your portfolio will increase over the decades and that you'll have a significant portfolio when you retire.

They nodded. Of course, the set-it-and-forget-it scenario was familiar. It's the gospel of traditional stock investing that most advisors sell their clients. Buy-and-hold, and in the end, you'll be rich, because your stocks will have appreciated in value, and that'll pay the bills.

There are a couple of problems with buy-and-hold investing, I said. The first is that it can leave a lot of profit on the table, as you've seen in the past year and probably saw during the 2008 financial crisis. I'm sure some of your stocks and stock funds went sky-high before each of those debacles—but you sold nothing, so those gains were all lost when the stock market tanked again.

The Cranes nodded vigorously. "There were some great years," John said. "For sure. And then, suddenly, the party's over."

But you didn't sell and take any profits, right? I asked. And I assume you weren't even looking at how much annual income your holdings produced.

"Well, no," said Jean. "We weren't at retirement age quite yet. We didn't need the money right away. We had time to wait for the market to recover."

She explained that the couple didn't follow public companies and the bond markets that closely, so they didn't feel confident trading in and out of different investments.

"Whoever has the kind of time to learn all the ins and outs, aside from pros like you?" she added. "Besides, they say trading in and out of stocks a lot, you end up losing money."

I chuckled. Ah, the ever popular "they," I said. What you're repeating is the advice nearly every advisor gives their clients. They plan to pay your retirement expenses by selling up to 4 percent of the assets each year, hoping that the market will continue to grow the values within the portfolio. Forever. Now *that's* a risky business.

I explained that besides leaving money on the table because you never sell, no matter how high the value soars, there's another problem with buy-and-hold investing. When you sell stocks or shares in a mutual fund that have appreciated over time, you may have to pay capital-gains tax on the profits.

From their reactions, I could see our new friends clearly got the point. Buying and holding securities across your entire working life can have serious drawbacks.

TOTAL RETURN VS. TOTAL REALIZED RETURN

Let me introduce a couple of terms to you, I said. Your buy-and-hold investment advisors probably talked to you about "total return." When they use that phrase, they mean your portfolio's gain in market value. Your portfolio is worth more because the market went up or less if it went down.

Let's say your total return was 15 percent one year, which sounds great. But unpack it, and 13 percent of it was market value growth. Only 2 percent was actual realized income, namely distributions and/ or capital gains. These are dividends your stocks paid out or interest on bonds.

A 2 percent realized return you can actually spend isn't very much! And always remember that you can't spend total return.

Change in market value does not equal spendable income. Change in total return doesn't mean you have more or less income, either. Unrealized gains are irrelevant in your quest for more retirement money that you can spend.

What you can spend is total realized return. That's what I focus on. It's the base income from your portfolio, plus the capital gains from any securities you sold profitably. Total realized return is what matters, because that's what you can spend—or better, can reinvest to make even more income.

"I've definitely heard that total-return spiel from my advisors," John said. "Good to know the difference between that and total realized return—which is what we need—actual spending money."

Exactly right.

MUTUAL FUNDS AND ETFS: MANAGED BY THE MOB

At this point, for the Cranes to understand why their portfolio wasn't meeting their needs, I needed to talk about how mutual funds and exchange traded funds (ETFs) work.

Mutual funds and ETFs have become the vehicles of choice for most investors today, possibly because this is what they could choose from in their 401(k) plans. Mutual funds were created in 1924, while ETFs got started in the 1990s.

Both mutual funds and ETFs invest in the same company shares, debt instruments, and government securities that are traded in the various markets, all wrapped up in well-diversified packages that significantly reduce risk. They're an excellent means of starter investing.

But the primary drawback of both fund types is that they are what I call "managed by the mob." That means the funds' value goes up or down depending on how all the investors in the market are feeling that day or that week. Mutual funds have managers, but those managers' decisions are really made on the whims of market participants.

"What do you mean?" John asked.

If there's a market downturn, I explained, mutual fund managers are forced to sell at a bad time to cash out panicked investors. Most ETFs still don't have managers, but the impact of shareholder demand is the same—the fund must sell securities if shareholders want out, even if it means taking a loss.

The reverse is also true: In good times, when more investors want in, mutual funds and ETFs are compelled to add more shares and buy more securities, even if they feel the shares are now overpriced. This all points up an important aspect of mutual funds and ETFs: The number of shares of the funds is unlimited—which is why they're known as *open-ended funds*.

Try to keep that open-ended fund idea in mind, I told the Cranes. I invest primarily in a product that *isn't* open-ended, and it's an extremely important distinction. I'll tell you more about it later.

THE TROUBLE WITH 401(K)S

The Cranes returned to their salads, appearing thoughtful for a few minutes. Then, John piped up.

"If mutual funds and ETFs have these disadvantages," he said, "why are they the most popular ways to invest? I feel like they're about all I ever heard of, and they include all forms of securities."

I put down my salad fork. Great question! I replied. The answer lies in the rules of the place you started investing: corporate 401(k) plans. That's where many people learn to invest—and mutual funds and ETFs are pretty much all that's offered in most 401(k)s. Those investing habits tend to stick with you later, even when you could invest in other ways.

Jean was listening intently. "Why *are* mutual funds and ETFs the main choices in 401(k)s, if they have these drawbacks?"

To understand why, you need a little history of 401(k) plans, why they were created, and the rules that govern them, I told the Cranes.

The 401(k) plan was created in 1978, mainly because corporate pension plans had become too expensive for companies to operate within market value rules. Just think if they had been income focused!

POINT YOUR PHONE'S CAMERA AT THE SQUARE ABOVE FOR MORE ON THE HISTORY OF 401(K) PLAN.

Regulators at the Employee Benefits Security Administration had big concerns about American workers making their own investment decisions and getting snookered. The general public got out of the markets after the market crash of 1929, so most people weren't knowledgeable about stock market investing.

How would the government ensure that these retirement accounts grew over time and provided for American workers in retirement? They did it by limiting your 401(k) investment choices so participants wouldn't be overwhelmed. Even today, the typical 401(k) plan only offers 8 to12 investment options, according to the Financial Industry Regulation Authority (FINRA).

Besides stock and bond mutual funds and ETFs, these options may include company stock, and annuities. A handful of highly trusted, big-name companies dominate the 401(k) mutual fund choices, too.

Regulators also worried about the fees investment firms charge, since those can eat into stock appreciation and erase gains. So they decreed that fees on 401(k) programs must be kept low.

If a mutual fund has smart managers making active moves in the stock market to take advantage of opportunities, that fund's fees would need to be higher than those of an ETF that's set to automatically own every equity on the Nasdaq, for example.

FOR MORE BACK-
GROUND ON THE 2
PERCENT FEE GUIDELINE,
SEE THE INVESTOPEDIA
ARTICLE ABOVE.

But regulators' dislike of high fees means you won't find an abundance of actively managed funds within 401(k) plans. It's also unlikely that you'll have choices that either generate much income or that are designed solely to produce income. Fund fees must stay under 2 percent by law. Most ETFs offered in 401(k) plans run on autopilot and produce low levels of income.

2% IS NOT A SOLUTION

At this point, I steered the discussion toward one of my biggest objections to investing solely in mutual funds, which typically have low yields when compared with the type of securities I'm going to be talking about.

If you're not familiar with yield, I explained, it's the amount of cash an investment generates in a year, as a percent of what you've invested.

Current yield is the total distribution per year divided by the current market value.

Investment pros like me call this cash distributions because some funds send shareholders a variety of things—dividends, interest, option premiums, and returns of capital. It's not just dividends.

For example, say your monthly statement shows your shares in a particular mutual fund are worth $5,000, and the fund pays you $225 per year. That's a current yield of 4.5 percent—and not something you'll see frequently in a mutual fund or in most ETFs.

Any idea what your yield is in your mutual funds? I asked.

John shrugged. "Not really."

Not wanting to make the Cranes feel stupid, I decided to stop and ask them about a figure I thought they'd surely know.

Well, let's back up a second. How much do you want to withdraw from your portfolio a year, as a percentage of total assets? I asked.

"I do know that," Jean said. "It's 4 percent, right? That's the figure they say to aim for. And that, hopefully, the portfolio grows more like 7 to 8 percent a year. That way, you can add more principal each year for investing, even after you take out the 4 percent." John nodded his agreement.

Actually, I said, that excess market value growth adds *absolutely nothing* to your invested assets. It's only paper profits.

Have you been able to stick to that 4 percent? I asked. Is that covering all your bills, including trips like these?

She looked a little rueful. "Not all the time," she admitted. "Not even in good markets."

I tapped my forehead with an index finger. OK, hold that thought about 4 percent withdrawals, I said. Let's go back to the question I asked you earlier—about what your IRA's annual yield is. The answer, typically, is less than 3 percent. In my experience, most don't even yield that much.

The Cranes looked shocked.

"What?" they said, nearly in unison.

Remember, those funds aren't designed to produce high income, I said. Most are not actively managed, as we've discussed. They're buy-and-hold investments you're hoping will appreciate in market value over time.

John pushed back his plate and sighed. "OK, I see what you mean."

My thoughts turned to his big stake in IBM stock and the other individual equities he'd accumulated.

When you own a large stake in a stock you like, such as your IBM shares I said, the problem of low yield can be even worse. All the "hot" tech stocks have low yields! Apple stock's yield was *half of 1 percent* (.50) in 2021.

I continued: The problem with the buy-and-hold investing approach is that your investments' total market value and $8 will buy you a nice latte. You can't spend market value! Unless you sell something, which often means either a tax bite or a loss of principal.

From the looks on their faces, the wheels were spinning fast inside the Cranes' heads.

The best thing about 401(k) plans is the company matching your money, I said. That's what turbocharges value growth in a company plan, that free cash. And you've already capitalized on that by rolling it over to an IRA.

John looked relieved. "At last, something we did right!" he said. "I always made sure to deposit enough to get all the matching money my employers offered."

That's great! I said. The matching money also helps overcome the fact that 401(k) management fees are deducted from the fund assets.

It didn't take John long to do that math. "I'm really not growing my income by very much each year—I'm barely breaking even!" he exclaimed.

Exactly, I said. And obviously, that's a problem.

WHY DRIPS ARE ALL WET

There was one more point I wanted to make about traditional retirement income programs.

Besides the low yield in most portfolios, I said, there's one other feature that causes a lot of problems and reduces your opportunities to profit from changing market conditions. Can I ask what you do with the dividends and other cash payouts that your investments generate each year?

He thought for a minute. "I'm pretty sure that I have those set to just be automatically reinvested into whatever security they came from," he said.

Exactly as I'd suspected.

I said, that's known as a DRIP—a Dividend Reinvestment Program. It's what most investors do with proceeds from their securities, so they don't have to make additional investment decisions every month. In fact, most brokerages automatically set new accounts to reinvest all income. I used to make a note every time I transferred a new account to kill the DRIP plan.

"Automatic" is not a word that should be in an investor's vocabulary. DRIP investing has four fundamental problems, I said, ticking them off on my fingers:

One is that it automatically reinvests in your existing securities no matter what their current price. If their share price is higher now, that purchase raises your average cost per share and reduces your yield.

Second, it increases the amount you have invested in each security. That can make your portfolio poorly diversified.

Third, it leaves you with no cash to use, either for expenses or new investment opportunities. With a DRIP, even if the portfolio produces enough for your expenses, you'd still have to sell securities to pay the bills. You've reinvested all your cash, so you can't withdraw it.

Finally, the artificial demand for shares caused by "dripping" increases the price you pay for the shares. That's mostly counterproductive, and now, someone has to decide what securities you're going to sell to pay expenses.

John and Jean exchanged a meaningful look. Clearly, they'd gotten a new perspective on how they'd invested for retirement—and a better idea of why their approach wasn't paying for their lifestyle.

A BETTER APPROACH?

At this point, I noticed Sandie discreetly raising an eyebrow at me. I tend to get up on a soapbox when it comes to the problems with traditional investing, and I talk peoples' ears off. She was signaling it was time to wrap up the critique.

From the beleaguered looks on their faces, it appeared the Cranes might be feeling a little overwhelmed. I cleared my throat.

Anyway, I said, you can probably tell this is a hot topic for me. No need to beat this into the ground. If you're interested, I wrote a whole book on this topic: *The Brainwashing of the American Investor*. It's available at The Retirement Income Coach website.

John spoke up. "I get what you're saying," he said. "But I don't know another way to invest that would be better, without being too risky. I'm not an investing genius, and I don't really want to turn investing into a full-time job."

His spouse nodded in agreement.

I absolutely understand, I said. There is a better way. It starts with switching your investment strategy from buy-and-hold to one that focuses on *growing income*. Just do what generates the most reliable income. Doesn't that seem like a smart goal in retirement?

Jean nodded. "Sure. But isn't that risky?"

I'm not advocating that you do anything crazy, I replied. I'm not a big risk-taker. What I do is probably less risky than owning mutual funds, ETFs, or individual stocks.

I do everything possible to minimize risk. Market value fluctuates, the same as it does with other securities, but we've all lived long enough to know that's the nature of marketable securities. All it takes is a little time to learn about a different class of investments than those you've been using.

Sandie's eyebrow had now reached maximum height. It was time to take a break from investment talk.

My wife thinks I'm monopolizing the conversation, I said. Why don't you take some time to digest what I've said, and if you want, I'm happy to meet with you once I'm back at my office.

There's a lot of details about my methods that would help you understand how I invest. And I *am* on vacation—or trying to be, I said, laughing. Would that be OK?

The Cranes nodded in relief. I'd given them a lot of new ideas, and they clearly needed some time to think. We moved on to other topics as we finished our dinner.

As it turned out, the Cranes were definitely interested in discovering a better way to invest. At the end of our cruise, they made an appointment to come visit me. They lived in Virginia, less than a day's drive from our home in coastal South Carolina. They planned a two-night stay to meet with me and learn about my income-focused investing approach.

FOUR: A Better Goal for Retirement Investing

B ACK AT HOME in South Carolina, the meeting-day weather was shaping up beautifully: sunny but not too warm. It was perfect for the post-meeting golf foursome we planned for the afternoon at the Oak Point Golf Club. I was up early, straightening up my basement office, making sure I had charts and other visual aids at hand, and putting away files and stray pens. Sandie did a quick round of decluttering, carting away a discarded sweater and a few stray dishes and mugs. I may work from home, but I still want to convey a professional attitude.

I'd noted that the Cranes had checked in the previous night at one of the most expensive hotels in our area, The Charleston Place Hotel in the historic downtown district. They may have had to sell assets to fund their Viking River cruise, but they clearly weren't hurting financially. I was happy to see that, because it meant they still had substantial assets I could help them grow—if they liked what they heard about my investing approach.

Suddenly, there was a knock on the door, and my train of thought came to a quick stop. The Cranes had arrived! I joined Sandie to greet them. We'd grown close in the course of our trip and getting to see them again was a bit like a family reunion.

Sandie gave them a quick tour of our home while I closed some computer files and got some interesting facts and figures together for the meeting. Then the three of them reappeared, equipped with mugs of coffee. I settled in behind my desk while they each found a comfy leather chair opposite me. Sandie politely excused herself, promising to rejoin us for lunch—she'd made a reservation at a club restaurant across from the 18th green.

We reminisced about how much we'd all loved our trip. After a bit of small talk, I steered the conversation to the reason they'd driven such a long way.

Ready to learn a different way to invest? I asked. I'd love to help you grow your retirement income so that you don't have to cash in any of your assets to pay for your next trip.

They both nodded vigorously. "That'd be a great first step," John said.

I'd like to start with the goal of my investing strategy, I said. I call it Income-Focused Retirement Investing, or IFRI.

THE DEFINITION OF INCOME-FOCUSED RETIREMENT INVESTING

I let this idea sink in for a minute.

"Aren't we already doing that?" John asked. "We have our retirement income."

Yes, I countered, but as you explained to me on the trip, it's not enough. It's not covering all the bills.

You're invested in various holdings—individual equities, mutual funds, bonds, and such—but they don't generate enough income. And over time, they've grown less diversified because of reinvesting income back into the same funds. Right?

Jean nodded agreement.

The premise of your investing now is to buy-and-hold, hoping that increased future market value will give you enough growth so that you can sell off assets to fund your retirement. You need to do that because their yield isn't enough to cover all your costs, I added, recapping what I'd taught the Cranes about traditional investing on our trip.

Buy-and-hold is *not* the strategy of my investing, I told them. Your portfolio's job is to create more income than you need—all the time. I invest and manage my investments with a goal of making my assets generate the most cash they possibly can, while minimizing financial risk.

I want enough cash to cover 4 percent payouts and then some. You need more for the extras like travel, right? Plus, I want cash left over to invest in additional assets. That'd be ideal, wouldn't it?

The Cranes nodded. "Of course," John said.

Here's how I define IFRI, I told them:

Retirement income and its growth shouldn't be negatively affected by stock market corrections, volatility, or higher interest-rate expectations. In fact, these events should help to grow both income and working capital even faster.

In a nutshell, my programs are so income-focused that my retired clients always have more than enough income to pay their expenses—and they're growing that income every year, regardless of market conditions.

There was a beat while the Cranes thought on this. Then, as I expected, they began to pick apart this definition to make sure they understood everything.

"It sounds like a dream that the stock market could go down and it doesn't affect your retirement income," said John. "And I kind of get how that could work from what you told us before . . . that market value doesn't matter in retirement as much as the amount of cash the assets generate—the yield.

"I can't wait to hear how you create a higher yield without risking the family farm, as they say. But first, explain the part about 'higher interest-rate expectations.' Why 'expectations? Isn't it higher interest rates that affect what the market does?"

I smiled. This is a question nearly all my prospective clients ask.

Have you ever noticed how the stock markets start gyrating when the news reports that the Fed is *thinking* about raising interest rates? I asked. It hasn't happened yet, but investors react to the rumor. Stock prices immediately start moving.

Sometimes, that rumored rate change doesn't even happen. But if it does, there's usually little reaction at that point, unless the change is more or less than anticipated. The change in investor attitudes is already "baked in." They reacted when they first heard it might happen.

That's why I say the *expectation* of higher interest rates shouldn't affect your retirement income. The actual interest-rate hike shouldn't, either.

"OK, I get that," Jean said. "Now talk us through the part where you're 'consistently growing your income.' Really, you should be able to see healthy, stable income from your investments every year, and not have down years like we had in 2022?"

I nodded.

That's exactly what my system has been accomplishing for decades, in good times and bad. I construct portfolios to keep spitting out reliable cash despite the ups and downs of stock prices and interest rates.

IFRI investing isn't about whether the market is up or down, I explained. It's about reaping profits and generating income. You can do at least one of those in all market conditions. Often, you can do both.

If you feel like you understand my IFRI definition, I added, I want to give you one more big idea. It's a mental mind shift in how you think about risk.

Jean seemed to take a big, deep breath.

"OK," she said. "How should we think about risk?"

A DIFFERENT WAY TO UNDERSTAND RISK

I was out of my chair, pacing around as I mapped out risks that really matter to investors—and those that don't.

There are two main types of risk in investing, I explained: financial risk and market risk. Other risks will affect these as well—inflation, political upheaval, war, and government lawsuits against companies, to name a few.

You've been taught to worry about market risk all your life—the fear that the stock market will go down, I said.

"Definitely true," Jean said.

But the stock markets go up and down routinely. That's why they call one complete circuit from down to up and back again a "market cycle."

I went on to explain that market risk isn't really a risk at all, though you might think of it that way. *Market cycles are the natural state of things.* There is no stasis in the business world. Economic conditions keep changing, and markets rise and fall. Yet we're taught to fear market downturns and pray they won't happen. Instead, investors should learn how to prepare for them—*and to take advantage of the opportunity!*

Why do I say it's not really "market risk"? Because if you simply hold onto your mutual funds or equities during a market downturn, nothing happens. Your portfolio is worth less on paper, but unless you sell, you've lost nothing.

John agreed. "That's true."

When you invest in the market, I explained, there are two basic "buckets" or types of investments, which serve different purposes: Either your investment is focused on income or on growth. With a market value focus, you tend to invest only for growth.

But if the equities you hold pay dividends, or the income-purpose securities you own pay interest or generate other cash payouts, those normally continue, even if the market value of those securities goes down.

And consider this: If their prices go up, the actual payouts generally don't change. Most income-purpose securities have contractual payments that can't be adjusted or omitted, and changes in stock dividends are mainly a function of company profitability.

People get upset when bond prices go down, for instance. But for someone who owns the bond, all that matters is the interest the bond pays and the repayment of the entire debt at maturity. Rarely does any of that change. It's locked in when you purchase the bond.

"I guess that's true," Jean admitted.

Next, I steered the conversation over to the other, more important type of risk for investors: financial risk.

Instead of worrying about market risk—which you've seen isn't really a risk but an inevitability—*worry about financial risk,* I told them. That's the type of risk *I* worry about.

Financial risk is the possibility that you'll lose money on an investment. You buy stock in a troubled company hoping their fortunes will improve but the company goes bust, leaving you with nothing. You buy a municipal bond, and that city declares bankruptcy. You invest in a mutual fund that owns all a foreign country's publicly traded equities, and their economy craters, leaving the fund nearly worthless.

Investing in a company's debt is always less risky than investing in that same company's common stock, or equity securities. That's in part because in a bankruptcy, debtholders are in first position for repayment. In contrast, if a stock becomes worthless due to a company's poor fortunes, equity investors typically get nothing. Equities are pieces of ownership of the company—and with ownership comes the greatest risk.

Buying a mutual fund that holds many equities is less risky than owning a handful of individual stocks. An unforeseen disaster at one company won't have a huge impact on a fund that owns hundreds of different stocks.

To limit financial risk, you need to scrutinize the viability of the companies or governments behind your securities. Are they vulnerable to a lawsuit? Is the company well-managed? These are the questions a good advisor asks as they seek to limit financial risk.

This is the risk I spend all my time thinking about and mitigating, I said. When you know how to limit financial risk, you can build a portfolio that'll pay your bills, even if the market tanks or interest rates spike.

INVESTING VS. SPECULATING

One last point about risk, I said. Know that everything I invest in is a proven, high-quality security with a long track record of income production. I don't engage in speculation. Getting a hot tip on a stock and "going with your gut" is not part of my investment approach.

To demonstrate what I meant, I handed the Cranes a list of speculative investment types. They include:

- Cryptocurrencies
- NFTs
- Penny stocks
- Precious metals futures
- Commodities, such as pork bellies
- Stock-shorting strategies
- Naked, or uncovered, options
- Hedge funds
- Angel investing in start-ups
- Initial public offerings (IPOs)

- Other illiquid vehicles, such as antiques, cars, individual homes, and collectibles

While speculators sometimes see big paydays, to me it's not worth the risk, I explained.

"Well, that's a relief," said Jean. "I don't have the stomach for any of this. I'd be too nervous!"

I don't speculate, I said. And I've never placed a client in any security I didn't own or trade for myself.

TIME TO DIGEST —— AND EAT

A quick look at the clock told me lunchtime was approaching.

I think that's enough information to load you up with for one morning, I said. Feel free to bring those handouts to lunch if you want to ask me about them. Lunch should give you time to digest what you've learned so far . . . and hopefully, to digest your lunch, too! Then we'll play a round of golf.

The Cranes rose from their seats. "Sounds great," John said.

PART II

6 Steps To More Retirement Money

S ANDIE REJOINED US and we piled into our SUV for a short drive to a restaurant on the 18th green at Cougar Point, in the Kiawah Island resort. I sensed that the Cranes needed some time before I unpacked more of my investing strategy, so we kept the chatter light at our patio table, catching up on what our children and grandkids had gotten up to since our cruise.

After we ordered our lunches—burgers for the Cranes, fish tacos for Sandie, a garden salad with chicken for me, and iced teas all around—Jean turned to me.

"I know we're going to meet back at your office to learn more about how you invest," she said. "But I'm wondering if you could give us a quick overview. Are there some basic rules you follow?"

There are six principles that guide what I do, I said with a smile. If you like, I can give you a quick introduction to them as we play. Then, I'll go into a lot more detail on each of those principles once we're back in the office tomorrow morning.

FIVE: The 6 Basic Principles of Income-Focused Retirement Investing

As I paid our check and we headed to the car, Jean said, "How about giving us one principle to think on as we drive over to the tee?"

Since my six principles have a distinct order to them, I knew right where to start.

#1: QUALITY MATTERS MOST OF ALL

You may have often heard the Ford slogan that "Quality Is Job One," I said. Well, quality is the first important principle in my investing strategy, too. In retirement, you don't want to invest in anything that's too risky, since you don't have time to earn more employment income. I'm always careful to choose proven, high-quality investments. I have a set of screens I use for that—I'll give you the whole rundown when we meet tomorrow. I'll go check in and get the carts.

Since we're all exercise nuts, we used push carts so we could talk as we walked the course. Sandie and I play golf more often than the Cranes, so we played a friendly game—no bets. We started talking again at the second tee.

"What's the next principle?" John said.

We talked about it a little bit on our trip, I replied. You'll remember that I asked you how diversified your portfolio was and whether you automatically reinvested income back into the same securities? Diversification is very important, so it's my second principle."

#2: DIVERSIFICATION IS ESSENTIAL FOR LIMITING RISK

This principle is a simple one to explain since most investors understand the need to diversify. You don't want to have too much invested in any one security or sector.

If you had only high-quality investments but they were all in the same industry or class, your portfolio would be vulnerable to big economic changes. For instance, if you were all in bonds, you'd never benefit from stock market rallies.

Diversification is essential to building a safe portfolio. That means high-quality positions in many types of securities, in both the equity and fixed-income markets. You need diverse types of investments to spread the financial risk. I rarely have as much as 3 percent of a portfolio in any one security.

The next principle I use is probably more of a new one for you than quality and diversification, I said. Let's wait to talk about it until we hit the 9th hole and take a pitstop.

#3: FOCUS ON INCOME PRODUCTION

There's a refreshment stand at the midway point on the course, so we stopped after the 9th hole to grab some ice water and take a quick breather.

Jean was clearly keeping track of the principles in her head. "OK, I'm ready for idea number three," she said. "You said it's a bit different from what we know?"

It is, I said. You'll remember on the trip, when I asked you about the yield you were seeing in your portfolio, and you didn't really know? And I told you I guessed it was probably 3 percent or less.

John perked up at this. "Actually, I looked into that when we got home," he said. "And you were right! Our securities don't generate much income at all."

This is where my system starts to look different from traditional investing, I told them. I build portfolios so that every security, stock or bond, generates some form of dependable income. It's not focused on what the market value of the underlying securities is at any given point.

There's more than one way for a portfolio to produce income, but the best way is to focus on *base income*. That's the money that comes from dividends on equity securities and interest on fixed-income securities. My retirement portfolio has at least 60 percent in income-purpose securities.

Quality and diversification are key elements, but income production pays the bills.

"Got it," said Jean.

You're halfway through the six basic principles I use, so give yourself a pat on the back! I said. Principle Four is another one that takes a little bit of new learning. Let's play a couple holes and then we'll come back to this. The last two are easy, I promise.

We rose, retrieved our "wheelies," and headed toward the 10th tee.

As we diversify into a variety of investments, our portfolio becomes like a department store, I said. It has securities representing the providers or producers of all manner of goods and services.

And how do department stores grow and prosper? I asked the Cranes. Certainly not by watching merchandise sit on the shelves and grow in value. They establish reasonable markups and take profits by selling their merchandise as soon as they can. That's our next principle: profit-taking.

#4 THE MAGIC OF TARGETED PROFIT-TAKING

So far in your lives, you've been buy-and-hold investors, I told the Cranes as I lined up a putt. As you know, that's not my approach. Like any other business, a portfolio should always reap profits and reinvest the proceeds in other productive assets. There's always something new to buy.

I use a flexible formula that rarely misses out on gains. If a security goes up in value to a certain point, I sell it and invest in something else.

John frowned. "Sounds like trying to time the market," he said. "I feel like every study ever done about this strategy finds that people who try to time the market end up earning less in the end."

We were walking to the next hole, but I stopped wheeling my cart to make a point. I thought you might say that—but what I do is nothing like market timing, I said. I don't care which way the market moves next or about the individual security I'm selling. Like a department store, I'm selling a product off the shelf and adding something new to my inventory.

More head-scratching from John. "But if it's going up, why not stay at least partially in that security?" he asked. "Maybe there's more upside there, and now you're losing out on it."

I resumed wheeling my cart. You make a good point, I said. There's a bit more to know about my approach that will clear this up for you. Why don't you hold that thought for tomorrow? I'll share more details on profit-taking then.

#5 UNDERSTAND MARKET CYCLES AND HOW TO MANAGE THEM

We walked toward the next hole.

"This is the most educational round of golf I've ever played!" Jean said, laughing. "You promised the next two points are easier, so I'm ready."

After we completed the hole, I moved on to Principle Five.

This fifth principal is almost going to be a review for you I said. We've already talked about market cycles, and the pain buy-and-hold investors feel when the markets go down or interest rates shoot up.

Market cycles are inevitable. Prices go up and down, and so do interest rates. These features are something to prepare for—and to take advantage of. Principle Five is simply to understand market cycles and how to manage them within your portfolio.

As your focus shifts from buy-and-hold to targeted profit-taking, you won't have the pain of leaving gains on the table when the market goes down. You take profits on upswings and reinvest in securities that boast a dependable yield.

You focus on income production by selecting securities that historically produce strong, reliable income. This allows you to ride out falling markets without having to sell securities to pay your bills.

We wheeled off toward the next hole. "I feel like there's still a lot to know about how, exactly, you find these great, income-generating securities," said John. "I'm looking forward to learning more tomorrow about how to invest so that a stock market downturn doesn't cause me pain."

#6 ASSESS PERFORMANCE

We got absorbed in our game on the rest of the back nine. After we played the last hole, I was ready to give the Cranes the final principle.

The last of my six principles is a simple one, I said. As with any retirement investing plan, it's important to stop periodically and analyze results. You wouldn't want to go on and on without seeing whether your strategy is succeeding or if there might be changes you should make to produce more income. I'll explain how I assess performance when we sit down tomorrow.

ONE INVESTMENT VEHICLE TO RULE THEM ALL

As we gathered up our gear and headed back to the car, John turned to me.

"Okay, we've got your six principles," he said. "Want to give us a hint on what, exactly, you invest in that gets you these stellar results?"

We put our clubs and other gear into the trunk.

Sure, I said. I invest primarily in a type of security known as closed-end funds, or CEFs. When we meet in the morning, that'll be the first thing we talk about—what CEFs are and why they're the best vehicles to use in implementing these six principles.

Jean weighed in: "Wow, I've never heard of those. Look forward to learning all about it!"

We dropped the Cranes back at our house, where they picked up their car and headed out for an evening of sightseeing on their own. I had plenty of preparation to do, to get ready for our morning meeting.

SIX: All About Closed-End Funds

THE CRANES TURNED up back at my home office early the next morning. It was their last day in town—they had to leave by late afternoon—and we had a lot of ground to cover.

Armed with coffee mugs, the Cranes settled in for our discussion of CEFs.

"I feel like we're finally getting to the action part of the learning," said Jean. "I can't believe you invest almost exclusively in a product I've never heard of—can't wait to find out how it works."

I smiled. Well, wait no longer! You have enough background now in my investing principles that you will understand why CEFs are my vehicle of choice.

I'll start with a simple definition of CEFs. Then, I'll explain how CEFs operate compared with mutual funds and ETFs, since you already know those. That comparison should give you a clear sense of CEFs' advantages.

CEFs DEFINED

Let's start with a basic definition of CEFs:

> CEFs are professionally managed, publicly traded investment companies. They raise capital through an initial public offering (IPO) of common stock. The proceeds are then invested according to the objectives of the fund. The fund operates as a "pass through" trust and must distribute at least 95 percent of its realized income to shareholders. A CEF has a board of directors, appoints an investment advisor, and employs a portfolio manager.
>
> After the IPO, no additional common shares are issued—which is why they're called "closed-end" funds. The number of shares is finite.
>
> CEFs are listed on national securities exchanges, where their shares can be bought and sold between investors throughout each trading day, just like individual company stocks. A typical CEF holds hundreds of different securities, helping to diversify your portfolio and lessen financial risk, compared with investing in individual securities. Currently, there are only about 500 CEFs to choose from compared to thousands of mutual funds and ETFs.

That's the bare bones of it, I told the Cranes. After the IPO, the CEF manager has a pool of money to invest in whatever the fund focuses on. CEFs can invest in anything from stocks and bonds—the most common categories—to real estate, other CEFs, various industrial sectors, you name it. Since I don't speculate, I tend to stick with CEFs that hold equities and debt securities, things that I feel do not have a lot of financial risk.

Just one other thing: Some CEFs take steps to increase the number of their outstanding shares by issuing purchase rights to existing shareholders. You may have experienced this with regular stocks that do similar rights offerings.

Each shareholder can maintain their ownership position by buying additional shares, or they can sell the rights and reinvest the money as they please. I never exercise my purchase rights—I sell them immediately and reinvest the cash selectively. Note that selling rights is the only way CEFs can raise their number of shares.

DIFFERENT KINDS OF CEFs

There are many flavors of CEFs, similar to how you can find many types of mutual funds, I said. There are CEFs that invest exclusively by type of security. They may hold only one class of debt security, such as government or corporate bonds.

Other CEFs invest in equities in one geographic region or country, such as Asia or Germany. Or hold only mortgages on multi-family properties. Still others hold only US dividend-paying stocks or only equities in a single sector, such as technology or energy. It's similar to the different choices you see with ETFs too.

But, with my approach to retirement investing, there are only two types of CEFs. Remember the two investing buckets? I asked.

"Right, I do," said Jean. "Growth purpose and income purpose."

Yes! I replied. In the big picture, the important thing is to understand whether a CEF's primary purpose in your portfolio is to create dependable income or to offer growth in its future share price. With CEFs, both income- and growth-purpose funds pay significant income. When we talk about asset allocation, I'll get into this in more detail.

CEFs VS MUTUAL FUNDS AND ETFs

Now that you understand what CEFs are, we can compare them with mutual funds and ETFs. What they have in common, as you can tell from their names, is they're all funds—vehicles that hold many securities, not just one.

But you'll recall that mutual funds and ETFs are open-ended funds, while CEFs are closed-end funds. Let's dig into how that difference changes how CEFs operate—because this is where the advantages become clear.

UNDERSTANDING THE ROLE OF NAV

To understand how CEFs operate differently than mutual funds and ETFs, you need to know about NAV—net asset value.

All funds have a NAV. It's the value of all the assets in the fund, minus any liabilities. Regardless of what the fund holds, at the end of each trading day, their closing value is set. Add up all those values, and you can calculate the fund's total NAV. Because the price of stocks and other securities fluctuates with the markets, a fund's NAV changes from day to day.

In open-ended funds, *the price of the funds' shares must remain equal to the NAV.* After the market closes each day, mutual fund managers reprice their fund's shares to equal its NAV. They do that to determine the price that days' buyers will pay. ETFs add and remove shares from the marketplace to create parity between the NAV and share price.

By contrast, a CEF doesn't make any attempt to align share price with the NAV, because it trades just like an ordinary company stock, where price is a function of supply and demand.

Think about an artist who sells a painting. They collect their sale fee from the art patron, and they're out. The painting might later be resold repeatedly, at higher or lower prices, but the artist isn't involved and doesn't benefit from it.

That's how CEFs work: They sell initial shares and invest the money in a portfolio of securities. But subsequent trading is between the shareholders—the trust itself isn't involved.

As a result, CEFs trade based on investors' opinions of that CEF's potential for either growth or income generation. That means that they rarely trade at the NAV, just like the individual securities they contain.

If investors are bullish on tech stocks right now, shares of your tech-focused CEF might trade at a premium. If not, they could trade at a discount. When interest went up so quickly in 2022, many income CEFs traded at a premium because their yields were so high, while their NAVs were actually falling.

This all means that with CEFs, sometimes, you can do something you can never do with mutual funds or ETFs: *Buy shares at a discount to the NAV.* You can buy shares with an underlying NAV of $10 for less than $10, when the CEF's shares are trading at a discount.

Because CEFs don't keep adding shares, the total number of shares in the market is more limited than you see with mutual funds and ETFs—fewer shares is also known as less liquidity. This often makes the CEF shares' price "spread" wider than you typically see with ETFs. Mutual funds always trade at the NAV, and ETFs always start the day at a share price equal to the NAV.

Just as with individual securities, the main force that determines CEF premium or discount is investor sentiment about the underlying securities in the CEF and how it's being managed.

One other key difference: CEF managers actively trade their portfolios, taking profits and establishing new positions, just as I do. Most ETF portfolios are not managed at all, and most mutual funds aren't actively managed, except in times of extreme greed or panic.

CEFs are more fully invested—and that means they have more opportunity to generate income and profits. CEF managers can also trade in securities that are less liquid than those found in ETFs and mutual funds—smaller issue-size bonds, for example.

THE LOWDOWN ON LEVERAGE

Because CEFs have more share stability, their managers can use leverage to improve their results. Roughly 85 percent of CEFs use leverage, according to the CEF Connect website. But what is leverage exactly?

Leverage is borrowing. Just as we use banks to finance our homes and automobiles, CEF managers borrow money to increase their pool of working capital. More money invested means more income opportunities for shareholders. Leverage in CEFs is no different from the borrowing that goes on in all public and private business operations throughout the world. Every business entity funds its operations with leverage.

In general, CEFs borrow money at low, short-term rates, repeatedly, over time. They invest that money in longer-term securities with yields higher than their borrowing cost. The difference between their borrowing cost and the realized profits is additional profit for shareholders. If they can't make a profit on the spread, they won't take on the debt.

There are two ways CEFs create leverage without diluting shareholders' interests:

- **SHORT-TERM LOANS AND OTHER DEBT:** The CEF gets a low-cost loan to buy more shares of securities, which produce a higher yield than the loan's cost.
- **PREFERRED SHARES:** The CEF sells preferred shares in the open market. In this case, if the dividend paid is lower than the amount earned, net income is increased.

Sound familiar? It's exactly what businesses do to grow their operations. Whichever way the CEF achieves leverage, the bottom line is that there's now more working capital to invest to generate distributions.

Almost all businesses operate using some form of leverage—they routinely take on corporate debt to grow the business. CEFs' business is creating income-productive portfolios.

In essence, *leverage magnifies the size of the securities portfolio under management—and, as a direct result, the amount of distribution income that can be paid to shareholders,*

Jean raised her hand. "Wait a minute," she said. "Using leverage sounds risky. Why doesn't this worry you, Steve? You said you don't like risky investments."

It's really no more risky, I replied, than any other business enterprise.

It's not that different from GM using a loan to build a new factory. It's all about screening and selecting the best-quality CEFs to invest in. We'll talk more in-depth about quality selection parameters shortly.

In my view, CEFs are the best way to get more—and more reliable—income from your portfolio. And as a retiree, that's what you need.

"How do CEFs do that?" asked Jean.

Let me explain.

HOW CEFS SOLVE THE INCOME-PRODUCTION PROBLEM

I mentioned in my CEF definition that these funds are structured as a pass-through trust. To keep that tax status, they must disburse 95 percent of their annual realized income to shareholders.

In my experience, most CEFs focus more on income generation than they do on growing their NAV, which is the metric mutual funds and ETFs focus on.

Think about it: If you have to disburse nearly all your net income, what can you use to grow your NAV? How can they compete on a market value growth basis with entities that disburse much less income?

Here are a couple examples of CEF mission statements:

- "The primary investment objective is to generate high current income, with a secondary objective to generate capital appreciation."
- "The Fund seeks total return with capital appreciation and high current income."

CEFs contain thousands of different securities of all types, sectors, and strategies, just like mutual funds and ETFs, but their payouts to shareholders are much larger.

For instance, let's look at my CEF "selection universes"—namely, the pre-screened sets of funds I create for my own investing. There's one universe for equity, or growth-purpose funds, one for tax-free income, and one for taxable income.

In September 2022, the average equity-focused CEF produced about 10 percent, the average taxable-income fund about 9 percent, and the tax-free funds around 5 percent.

With typical mutual fund and ETF yields less than 3 percent, it's not hard to see why CEFs are better for an income-focused investor.

THE (LONG) HISTORY OF CEFS

"So," said John, "are CEFs something new in the world of investing? That would explain why I've never heard of it."

Absolutely not, I replied. In fact, CEFs have been around longer than mutual funds and much longer than ETFs. The first CEF appeared in the US in 1893, some 30 years before mutual funds. The Investment Company Act of 1940 codified the rules for how CEFs operate.

In a way, CEFs are the granddaddy of all the fund types. They have a longer track record than any other—and there are several screener websites like CEF Connect that allow you to track performance over long periods of time in order to help you select top-quality CEFs. Screener websites allow you to sort securities based on different characteristics, like yield, price, leverage, and management company.

WHY THERE ARE NO CEFs IN 401(K) PLANS

John shook his head. "It's hard to believe I've never heard of CEFs before this, given how long they've been around," he said.

I explained that the ignorance is likely because CEFs aren't permitted in 401(k) plans.

"Why is that?" Jean asked.

It has to do with the fee structure, I explained. Because CEFs are more actively managed than mutual funds and ETFs, they are more expensive to run. Sometimes fees are in line with the 2 percent cutoff regulators have for 401(k) investments—but they can be higher.

They also may use leverage and have fewer shares outstanding than ETFs' and mutual funds' unlimited shares. So the whole investment class of CEFs is virtually excluded.

When you first began investing through 401(k) plans, no CEFs were in the selection menu, I said. When you rolled that into an IRA, you didn't know what other options you might have, outside of individual stocks and bonds, right? You just kept investing as you always did.

It's a common situation, and one of the reasons CEFs are less well-known. But for those who do know them, CEFs' income-generating power makes them a terrific vehicle for creating reliable retirement income.

7 BENEFITS OF CEFs

To sum it up, there are seven reasons CEFs are my investment vehicle of choice:

1. **REGULAR INCOME DISTRIBUTIONS:** CEFs are profit focused, and most make monthly distributions. Nearly a third may make additional special distributions of capital gains at year-end.

2. **STRONG DIVERSIFICATION:** CEFs invest in all varieties of tax-free and taxable investment securities. Anything that can be invested in individually can be found inside a CEF, even index-type investments.

3. **FULLY INVESTED PORTFOLIOS:** Since CEFs don't have to hold a reserve, that means more money can be invested, which leads to higher income and profit potential.

4. **INCOME FOCUSED:** Even equity CEFs offer yields three to four times higher than other forms of equity investing.

5. **ACTIVELY MANAGED:** CEF managers trade actively throughout the day.

6. **RIGHTS OFFERINGS:** Rights present shareholders with the opportunity to add to their positions at a specific price.

7. **LOWER SHARE PRICES:** Many sell below $10 per share, which some consider a danger sign in individual stocks. But I can buy stocks like Amazon and Apple that go for hundreds per share for $10 or less by buying a CEF that contains them.

Now that you understand the benefits CEFs offer an income-focused investor, there's one more aspect of CEFs to consider.

THREE DIFFERENT TYPES OF CEFs

There are three types of CEFs, in terms of what securities are inside, their purpose in your portfolio, and their tax consequences. Just to refresh your memory, I have a separate selection universe for each type of CEF. If I'm looking to buy an equity CEF, for example, I've already got a list of all the suitable candidates. I periodically update these lists to keep them current. What are the three types of CEFs?

- **TAXABLE INCOME:** These CEFs hold all forms of income-purpose securities other than tax-free municipal bonds. Examples include corporate bonds, real estate, loans, preferred stock, and mortgages. Their primary purpose is income production.

- **EQUITY SECURITIES:** These CEFs hold stocks traded on any stock exchange. Although they pay serious income, their primary purpose is to produce growth through profit-taking.

- **TAX-EXEMPT BONDS:** These CEFs hold municipal bonds, usually hundreds of them in a single fund. While there are state-focused Muni-bond CEFs for California, New Jersey, and New York, I prefer more diversified tax-exempt CEFs. They're one of the least financially risky types of investments and a reliable income producer, except when interest rates are rising quickly.

Either of the income-purpose CEF types will present profit-taking opportunities fairly often, while the equity or growth variety is expected to produce frequent profits during any prolonged market rally.

One final twist: Some CEFs are "hybrids," in that they contain a mix of both stocks and income-purpose securities. Hybrid funds with more than 35 percent in stocks are considered part of the equity-security universe.

Remember that department store your portfolio became when you first began to diversify? With CEFs, we create a much larger business model for your investments. It's more like we've got a major shopping center on our hands—one with a stake in nearly everything going on in the world economy.

Now that you understand the basics of what CEFs are, I said, I want to circle back to the six investing principles I taught you.

Let's go more in-depth on each one so you can see how CEFs are a perfect fit for each aspect of my investment approach. I think you'll see why I used them for decades for my clients and still use them in my own portfolios.

SEVEN: Principle I: Quality

Finding Quality Investments That Produce Reliable Income

WAS CURIOUS HOW much the Cranes had retained from our quick overview on the golf course about the six principles I use for investing, so I threw them a pop quiz. What's the first—and most important—principle I taught you for investing? I asked.

Jean got there first. "Quality," she said.

Exactly, I replied. If you don't choose good-quality investments, you won't have reliable, consistent income.

So how do I decide if an investment is high quality? I like to use CEF Connect for this analysis. For an example, I'll refer to what I discovered when looking at two CEFs: HPI, the John Hancock Preferred Income Fund, and the Gabelli Equity Trust (GAB), both of which I've been investing in for many years. Let's walk through my seven quality criteria. I'm going to talk about their stats on CEF Connect and walk you through the numbers. Feel free to look up this or any other CEF online on the platform of your choice. But this will show you what I look for.

I. AGE OF FUND

My guideline is that I don't include any funds with less than five years' history in creating my selection universes. Most of the CEFs I invest in have been around far longer—the average is over 18 years. HPI has been around for 20 years, GAB for 37.

Why is age an important quality screen? Because you need at least five years' worth of data to review to understand how that fund performs over time. I want to look at the consistency of their distributions.

New funds may focus on a strong industry or boast high yields, but they simply don't have proof yet that their managers produce consistent distribution rates suitable for retirees. So, I'm not interested.

The exception to this rule is that sometimes, an older fund merges into one with a new name. In this case, you can look at the previous fund's track record to review manager performance.

PRINCIPLE 1: QUALITY

2. VOLATILITY

It may sound weird to you, but I like to see volatility in CEFs' share prices. Ideally, when you review the long-term chart showing stock price relative to the NAV, you'll see it's traded at a discount and at a premium. It will have trended down during the '08 financial crisis, up during 2021's super-low interest rates, and down again in '22. This is what I want to see, and, if you look at their charts, both GAB and HPI have it.

Why is volatility good? Price fluctuation is your opportunity to buy low or sell high—or possibly, to just sell a bit higher than you bought. More on that coming up, when we go in-depth on profit-taking.

If there's no volatility in the fund's share price, there's less profit opportunity. And that's no fun at all.

3. FUND OBJECTIVES

We have a goal to see growing, high levels of income. You want to find CEFs with managers that share your goal. For example, HPI is an income CEF, so the stated objective is to invest 80 percent of its assets in preferred stocks, mostly investment grade. Clearly, their top priority is income production. Value growth is secondary.

GAB is a growth CEF. Its objective is a long-term increase in capital, with income as a secondary goal. But note it's still yielding nearly 11 percent!

4. CURRENT YIELD

Here's where the quality evaluation gets truly practical. If you can't buy a CEF at a price that gives you a solid yield, you shouldn't buy it.

My minimum yield target is 6 percent for taxable-income CEFs, 5 percent for equities, and 4 percent for tax-free funds. Quite often, I'm able to get substantially higher yields. If you think this kind of cash flow is hard to come by, it's not. In spring 2023, there were over 200 CEFs yielding from 6 to 10 percent. In addition, there were 40 tax-free CEFs yielding an average of nearly 5 percent.

What will happen as things change? Picture the scales of justice. Since the distribution rate of most CEFs is constant, if the price goes up, the yield goes down proportionately. As of spring 2023, you could buy both GAB and HPI yielding over 10 percent.

As interest rates stabilize, or appear to trend lower, the NAVs start to rise, along with share prices, so yields move lower. All income-purpose CEFs rise in NAV with falling interest-rate expectations (IRE).

Current yield varies with IRE and is always a possible deal-breaker. If the yield is below 6 percent without a good reason—such as a history of special year-end distributions, for instance—then it no longer qualifies as a good-quality investment. You've got to be able to buy at a price that gives you the yield needed to keep building your portfolio.

5. NUMBER OF SECURITIES

The whole point of investing in funds—instead of individual stocks and bonds—is that they mitigate risk by owning many different securities. That means you need to look up how many securities a CEF holds. You can see that HPI has 136, and GAB has 703.

My minimum number is 50. If the CEF holds preferred stock or bonds, I'd like to see many more. The average number of securities held in CEFs in my equity universe is 250; in the taxable-income category it's 470, and in my tax-free CEFs, it's 350. Obviously, the more different securities there are, the more insulated you are from problems within any single entity.

6. CONCENTRATION BASED ON TOP 10 HOLDINGS

Next, look at whether a CEF's largest holdings have too much weight. In other words, how much of the total is concentrated in the 10 largest fund positions? This tells you whether the CEF is diverse enough to properly shield you from risk.

Add up the percentages of the top 10 and you get a good, quick yardstick of portfolio concentration. HPI had 20 percent of the fund invested in the top 10, and GAB had 24 percent.

My guideline is that I don't want to see more than 40 percent of the fund invested in the top 10. If it's higher than that, the other positions will all be too small.

Remember, heavy concentration means higher risk. In this case, the 10 largest holdings make up less than 25 percent of the total holdings, with less than a third of the positions over 2 percent.

7. LONG-TERM DISTRIBUTION HISTORY

This final metric is one of the most important quality features. How long has this CEF been paying distributions? How consistent are they over the years, especially in years when the stock market crashed, or interest rates soared? Consistent distributions are a good sign.

One other thing to look at is how *frequently* the fund issues distributions. Is it monthly, quarterly, or annually? Monthly is best, as that means you get your hands on the cash sooner and can reinvest it faster, accelerating the pace at which you generate additional income. HPI shows a very stable monthly pattern.

Another aspect to look at in distribution history is whether the fund issues special distributions.

Special distributions are more common with equity funds—HPI is an income fund and hasn't had any since '07. GAB has declared 20 special distributions over the past 30 years. It's always great to see that, as it's a sign that the fund takes its income payments to shareholders seriously. And who doesn't like an unexpected payout?

CREATING HIGH QUALITY SELECTION UNIVERSES

Once you understand all seven of these quality screens, you're ready to start building "selection universes"— spreadsheets listing CEFs that are income focused and fit all, or most of, the quality criteria.

These guidelines are flexible. Sometimes, I make a judgment call that a CEF should be in my universes, even though it falls short on one or two criteria. This should never be done in small portfolios.

Why do I say universes, and not just one universe? You'll remember that there are three basic types of CEFs: taxable, tax-free, and equities. Use your quality screens within each category to identify the best choices.

One final note about screening CEFs for quality: If you ever read a CEF's description and don't understand it, even after some cursory research, don't invest in it. Some CEFs use complex or unusual investing strategies. If I can't figure out what they're up to, I pass. Only invest in securities and with strategies that you understand.

ADDITIONAL QUALITY SCREENS FOR INDIVIDUAL STOCKS AND BONDS

"This is great," John said. "I feel like I'm starting to really get a sense of how you limit risk in your investing and figure out which CEFs to invest in.

"One question—could I apply these quality rules to individual stocks and bond funds I own? You're making me wonder if the ones I inherited are good investments to stick with for the future."

You can, but you will have to do more homework than you do evaluating a CEF. In addition to the general quality rules above, you'll want to look at different specifics, depending on whether you're evaluating an equity or a fixed-income security.

BONDS: RATINGS AND MATURITIES

Individual bonds are fairly easy to scrutinize, because they have ratings you can review, I explained. Three organizations issue bond ratings: Moody's, Standard & Poor's, and Fitch. AAA bonds are the most attractive to many, but because they're so highly rated, they typically pay the lowest interest rates.

I used to invest in individual municipal bonds when I first began. But I started using CEFs quickly. They're just more effective for managed portfolios.

I'm guessing that your only income-purpose holdings are in mutual funds and/or ETFs, I told John. I'm confident that they're prudently selected, even if they're not actively managed. I can't remember the last time I saw an individual bond in a new client's portfolio.

All the complications associated with owning individual bonds are dealt with for us by active CEF managers. Using research tools at CEF Connect, you can dig into what's inside your bond funds as you wish.

STOCKS: DIVIDENDS, DEBT, AND RATIOS

Today, individual stocks take more legwork to evaluate than bonds, because sadly, Standard & Poor stopped providing a monthly quality rating guide. Morningstar and other rating agencies offer stock ratings, but their ratings don't cover what analysts call basic fundamentals. Instead, they compare a stock's market value performance to that of other companies in the same category or sector. In some cases, paying dividends to shareholders is considered a negative attribute!

Without ratings that analyze a stock's underlying fundamentals, you'll need to dig into the company's SEC filings. Start by looking at two metrics:

- **PRICE-TO-EARNINGS RATIO:** For this metric, compare a stock's share price with its net earnings. If the price-to-earnings (P/E) ratio is high—as it generally is in Nasdaq issues—it could mean the stock is overpriced. Conversely, a low P/E ratio means the stock may be undervalued.
- **DEBT TO EQUITY RATIO:** This ratio shows you the extent to which a company uses leverage. It compares the company's total debt liabilities—loans, notes due, lease payment obligations, and the like—to the value of all company shares. The higher the debt is in comparison to the stock's total value, the more financial risk for shareholders.

Did that ring a bell? As I said before, leverage is everywhere. CEFs only use it to purchase more securities, not employee bonuses.

There's more you can look at. I recommend checking dividend history, profitability, and any potential government lawsuits. It's a bit of work, but these two key metrics plus the dividend history give you a useful snapshot of company health.

QUALITY IS JOB ONE

There's a reason quality is my first screen: If you don't select quality funds to invest in, you won't achieve your income goals. It's tempting to ignore some of the quality elements when you get a hot tip on a new fund. *Resist.* Trust me, most often you'll end up sorry.

"Got it," John said. "But before we leave this quality topic, I have to say I'm surprised that you didn't name the amount of leverage as a quality metric. Really, you don't look at that at all?"

I don't. The amount of leverage is limited to 50 percent max by law. Most funds don't use that much. And as we've discussed, leverage is important for increasing distributions.

If I trust CEF managers in terms of what they invest in, based on their track record, I also trust them to use leverage responsibly. After all, leverage contributed to those 20 years of consistent distributions from HPI, for one.

"I see what you mean," said Jean.

I was ready to shift to the next metric. We talked about diversification as I walked through these quality screens. I said, now, let's take a closer look at how to lessen risk in your portfolio with what I call "offensive" diversification.

EIGHT: Principle 2: Diversification

A New Approach to an Iconic Strategy

B Y NOW, YOU'RE familiar with diversification, I said to the Cranes. To review: Diversification is a process that limits the amount of working capital in individual securities, security sectors, geographic regions, particular industries, or investment strategies. The goal is to spread financial risk.

You don't want to invest all your retirement money in, say, Berkshire Hathaway, even though it's a great company with an impressive track record. Why? Well, ask yourself what happens the day Warren Buffett dies. You don't want all your eggs in one basket, even if that basket currently looks wonderful.

To achieve strong diversification, you need a sharp sense of how risky different investments are. With the help of the members of my Facebook CEF Groups, I've organized all 29 CEF types into a financial-risk pyramid. Look at the pyramid, then I'll walk you through all the investments mentioned and why I've placed them as I have.

THE CLOSED-END-FUND RISK PYRAMID

Here's where the different investment types reside on the risk pyramid:

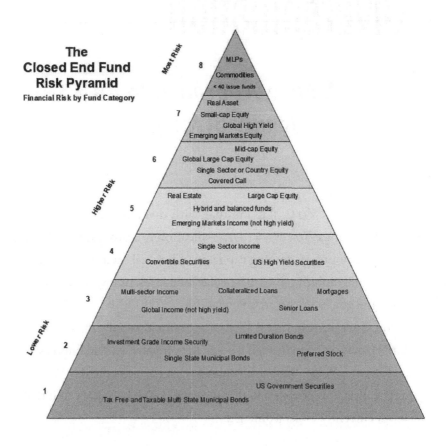

The Closed End Fund Risk Pyramid

Financial Risk by Fund Category

Most Risk

8 — MLPs
Commodities
< 40 issue funds

7 — Real Asset
Small-cap Equity
Global High Yield
Emerging Markets Equity

6 — Mid-cap Equity
Global Large Cap Equity
Single Sector or Country Equity
Covered Call

Higher Risk

5 — Real Estate / Large Cap Equity
Hybrid and balanced funds
Emerging Markets Income (not high yield)

4 — Single Sector Income
Convertible Securities / US High Yield Securities

3 — Multi-sector Income / Collateralized Loans / Mortgages
Global Income (not high yield) / Senior Loans

Lower Risk

2 — Investment Grade Income Security / Limited Duration Bonds
Single State Municipal Bonds / Preferred Stock

1 — US Government Securities
Tax Free and Taxable Multi State Municipal Bonds

"This is an interesting visual," Jean said. "I think I understand most of these investment types, but not all."

OK, I said. Let's run it down, starting with the solid, safer foundation. In overview: Down in the more stable, less risky bottom of the pyramid are four levels of income-purpose securities. The top four levels of the pyramid cover mostly equity investments since they're generally riskier than bonds. Let me briefly explain each type and its risks:

Level 1: Safe as it gets

US GOVERNMENT SECURITIES
These are the gold standard for bonds that pay interest and don't default, ever. Yields are usually modest—but boy are they reliable.

TAXABLE AND TAX-FREE MULTI-STATE MUNICIPAL BONDS
As long as the fund's muni-bond holdings are spread among many municipalities, muni-bonds are historically the next best thing to federal bonds.

Level 2: Still a safe investment

LIMITED-DURATION BONDS
These are considered low risk because even if you're at a low yield and interest rates rise, your bond matures soon, at face value. Then, you can reinvest in something with a better yield.

INVESTMENT-GRADE INCOME SECURITIES

These are well-rated US corporate bonds. An S&P rating from AAA to BBB, or a Moody's rating from Aaa to Baa3 means that they're investment-grade securities with a strong capacity for paying their commitments.

These highly rated bonds' yields tend to be lower, so there's a trade-off.

SINGLE-STATE MUNICIPAL BONDS

Not as diversified as a broader portfolio of muni bonds, but, hey, there's only been one major muni-bond default in the past 50 years.

PREFERRED STOCK

Preferred stocks provide more frequent distributions than bonds, and are sometimes convertible into common stock. They are also in a better position in a bankruptcy because holders get paid back ahead of common stockholders.

Level 3: Bond types with a little more risk

MULTI-SECTOR INCOME

Corporate bonds carry more risk than government bonds, but staying well-diversified across industries provides a measure of safety.

GLOBAL INCOME (NOT HIGH YIELD)

Global companies that can attract investors to their bonds are usually larger organizations in solid financial condition. If you want global diversification, this is the safest way to go.

COLLATERALIZED LOANS

These are considered safe because of the collateral. If the lender defaults, you're made whole by an asset sale. It's hard to go too far wrong.

SENIOR LOANS

Senior loans are a priority, ahead of other company debt. In case of trouble, senior notes will be the last debt a company stops repaying.

Level 4: Riskier bonds are still safer than equities

SINGLE-SECTOR INCOME

These funds contain bonds in a single industry, say tech or utilities. They're not as safe as more diversified, bond based CEFs due to the sector exposure, but they're still bonds.

CONVERTIBLE SECURITIES

Convertibles have an option to change the investment from one form to another. Most commonly, these are bonds or preferred shares that holders can convert to common stock. If the stock has moved up enough in price to make it profitable, you could elect to convert, then sell your shares for a profit. Prices for income CEFs containing convertibles tend to move more with the stock market than the bond market.

US HIGH-YIELD SECURITIES

Also known as "junk bonds," these are lower-rated corporate securities than the investment-grade securities in Level 2. They're generally from smaller companies with less solid financials, so they must offer higher yields to attract investors.

Despite what you might recall from the junk-bond fiasco of the '80s, today these securities rarely default—and they can offer substantial income.

Level 5: Less risky equity funds

LARGE-CAP EQUITY

Stick with a diverse array of big, successful, blue-chip American corporations—the kind with many shares trading—and you'll rarely experience serious financial difficulties.

HYBRID AND BALANCED FUNDS

Some CEFs are a hybrid or "balanced fund" of stocks and bonds. In this case, if 65 percent or more of the securities are income purpose, I include it in the income bucket.

These CEFs are less risky than equity-dominated funds.

EMERGING MARKETS INCOME (NOT HIGH YIELD)

Things change quickly in emerging markets. Also, bond rules can differ outside the US, so managers have to be careful. Remember, these are debt securities of companies whose equities are not as strong as those of established companies representing major world economic powers. These are one of two CEF types that could be more financially risky than top-shelf equity CEFs.

REAL ESTATE

Owning a diversified fund of real estate holdings is considered a solid investment. They're just not making any more land. REITs—which own many real estate holdings and must meet several requirements— are often used within these CEFs, making them particularly attractive.

REITs are similar to CEFs in structure and operation. I've had good experience with them individually, but a better experience when they're inside real estate CEFs.

Level 6: Some equity types worth a look, depending on your risk appetite

MID-CAP EQUITY

Take a bit more risk with US companies that aren't as large or well-established as large-cap firms and may have a more modest number of shares in the market.

GLOBAL LARGE-CAP EQUITY

If your fund invests in only the biggest, most successful global companies—Dior, Alibaba, Samsung, and the like—that fund is less risky than a more broad-based global equity fund. Few of these companies pay serious dividends, so these CEFs usually generate distribution income from trading.

SINGLE SECTOR OR SINGLE COUNTRY EQUITY

As we've discussed, it's always riskier to invest in a single industry's stocks than in a broadly diversified fund. And relying on the economy of a single country, well, think about how Greece defaulted on its debt to the International Monetary Fund in 2015 and the S&P declared Venezuela in selective default late in 2017. Even in the US, politicians have recently used threats of default as a political bargaining tool.

Additionally, CEF fund managers are wary of the risks in communist states, such as China, and you should be, too. Level six funds are the transition between relatively safe equities and higher-risk opportunities.

COVERED CALL AND BUY/WRITE FUNDS

If you're not familiar with these strategies, they involve profiting from options trading. The managers can make money in two different ways. First, they enter into a contract with a buyer to sell a security in their portfolio at a price higher than their cost. They get a premium for offering that contract—say it's $2.

If the buyer exercises the "call" and buys the security, there's a realized capital gain.

In addition, if the call expires without execution, the manager can sell another call and collect the premium again, with a potential capital gain later.

Buy/write sounds like exactly what it is. First the stock is purchased, then a call contract is "written."

Level 7: Higher-risk equities

REAL ASSETS

Ever tempted to buy some diamonds or gold bars and stash them in a safe-deposit box when the price is shooting up? Don't. If you're interested in metals, you can own a diversified CEF that contains gold and other real-asset specialty stocks that pay nice dividends instead. This is way less risky but still speculative compared with other CEFs.

SMALL-CAP STOCKS

These tend to be more financially risky than bigger-company shares. Smaller companies usually have fewer lines of business, which means they're more likely to see trouble in an economic downturn. They're also less likely to pay dividends, so they're less valuable to an income-focused investor.

GLOBAL HIGH-YIELD FUNDS

Funds like these are problematic because the public perception is that global companies aren't as high quality as US companies. That perception keeps global securities undervalued. In this case, the fund's yield is a function of those elevated financial risks. This is the second type of income-purpose CEF that's riskier than your typical equity CEF portfolios.

EMERGING MARKETS EQUITIES

Remember, the biggest foreign economies, such as China and India, are included in global stock funds. That leaves countries like Bangladesh, Iran, or South Africa in this category, countries often susceptible to social unrest. They're also smaller economies, so they're naturally riskier.

"Now this is fascinating," John said. "I can remember being offered fund options like those last two—global high-yield and emerging markets—in my 401(k) plans at work. They were sold as funds that could be countercyclical to what US stocks would do, so maybe they'd go up if US equities were down."

That might have been true once, I replied, but in our increasingly global economy, it's less and less so. All the big companies are now global—all the big US companies sell overseas, and vice versa. What affects the US tends to ripple through markets around the globe.

Level 8: Three super-risky things you should simply avoid

COMMODITIES FUTURES

This is betting on the future price of wheat or cotton, for instance. Commodity prices are affected by many factors you can't control, from the weather to fluctuating consumer demand. I never go there!

ANY CEF CONTAINING < THAN 40 SECURITIES

Forty securities are not enough diversity within the fund's portfolio, as we've discussed.

MASTER LIMITED PARTNERSHIPS (MLPS)

This is a common investment structure for the oil and gas industry. As such, they're single-industry focused and vulnerable to wild swings, depending on the price of gas and other geopolitical factors. Historically, I've experienced the most losses in my investing career in MLPs.

TAKE YOUR OWN RISK TEMPERATURE

Now that you understand the various risk levels of the different types of CEFs, you can create a diversification strategy that's within your comfort zone. As retirees, you'll want to be on the less risky side.

The big takeaway: A company's equities are riskier than all of that same company's fixed-income securities.

"This is super-useful information," said Jean. "I've never had all the different types of stock and bond investments broken down for me in quite this much detail. But I'm curious, do you have some diversification rules, like you did for quality?"

Of course, I do, I said with a smile. I've got rules and guidelines for everything.

THE RULES OF "OFFENSIVE" DIVERSIFICATION

Offensive diversification doesn't just mitigate risk, it actively opens more profit opportunities and helps create more even cash flow throughout the month. Only certificates of deposit (CDs) or money market funds carry zero risk. Beyond those safety-net holdings, you want to spread your risk across many categories.

Imagine you have 50 securities holding 2 percent each, or you have 100 securities holding 1 percent. Which scenario is most likely to generate a profit next week? Probably, the 100 security portfolio. You simply have more horses in the race.

Here are the five ways you need to diversify to achieve offensive diversification:

I. BY ASSET ALLOCATION BUCKET

Begin with the big picture: How much of your working capital do you want in your growth-purpose bucket and in the income-purpose bucket? This decision shapes all the other choices.

The percentages you should choose depend on your age and risk appetite. If you're in your 40s, you can put more money in the stock market. You have time to earn more salary—and you can wait out market downturns to reap future market value gains.

By the time they're within 10 years of retirement, most investors have between 30 percent and 40 percent in stocks, as their focus shifts to income production. If your money is still in a 401(k) plan, you should roll it over to an IRA as soon as possible, where you can choose investments that offer higher income.

Right now, for example, I'm 77 and have just 35 percent of my portfolio in equity CEFs.

If you're going to over-weight one bucket, it's better to be temporarily over-invested in the income bucket. Don't ever do it for market-timing reasons, though. Remember, nobody succeeds at timing the market.

2. BY INDIVIDUAL POSITION SIZE, IN BOTH DOLLARS AND PERCENTAGES

No more than 5 percent of working capital should be invested in any single position, except in very small portfolios. Otherwise, your portfolio quickly becomes too concentrated.

Personally, I don't like to go over $50,000 in a single position. That's 5 percent of a $1 million portfolio. I don't feel comfortable with that. You'll need to establish your own personal comfort zone.

I once managed a $7 million account, and of that, there were only three positions in which I committed over $100,000. The few large positions were in very low-risk bond trusts.

3. BY STARTING POSITION WORKING CAPITAL

If we don't want more than 5 percent in any position, it's important not to plop 5 percent into a security right off the bat.

If you do, you have no room for additional purchases if the share price falls. Preserve the option to lower your cost basis by buying additional shares for less later.

For instance, if a person has a $300,000 investment portfolio, 5 percent is $15,000. I'm not going to invest more than $4,000 in any one security for them. If the market goes down, I'd have $11,000 more I could use to purchase cheaper shares before reaching the 5 percent cutoff.

Besides the 5 percent upper limit, I also have a floor. I don't like to start with less than $2,000 in any one security. I might bend this rule a little for very small portfolios, but I never buy less than 100 shares of any CEF.

If you have a small portfolio, make sure you regularly recalculate to keep your positions under 5 percent. Tiny positions should probably be sold and consolidated into something with a higher yield, and positions over 5 percent should be reduced at the first profit-taking opportunity... or even at a loss, if they're seriously too large.

4. BY SECTOR OR TYPE

This rule is simple: No more than 15 percent of working capital should be invested in any one sector. As I write this, tech stocks are taking a beating, for instance. Staying diversified across industries allows you to experience—and benefit from—their ups and downs. You should have some positions in all sectors, if possible.

5. BY FINANCIAL RISK

No more than 10 percent of your working capital should be invested in the top two tiers of the risk pyramid. If your portfolio is small—say, less than mid-six figures—you should have nothing invested in higher-risk securities.

Hopefully, you can see that applying all five of these screens to your portfolio makes you well diversified. Your portfolio should be well-insulated from risk and offer many opportunities for capital growth and income production.

BUT AREN'T CEFS ALREADY DIVERSIFIED?

"Those rules are really useful to know, and make perfect sense," Jean said. "But why do we have to know so much about it, when quality CEFs are already well diversified?"

Because there are many different flavors of CEFs, I said. You wouldn't want to only have CEFs that are portfolios of US T-bills, right? Then, there wouldn't be anything in your growth-purpose bucket. It's important to select CEFs with different asset classes and investing approaches.

For retirees, we know the income bucket is critical. So, let's do a deep dive into that core principle next.

NINE: Principle 3: Income

It's the Focus of Retirement Investing

T'S A SIMPLE truth that retirees need money to live on. You can't buy groceries with market value—only with cash. That's why every CEF in your portfolio must generate significant income, whether the CEF holds fixed-income securities or growth stocks.

Fixed-income securities are bonds, mortgages, T-Bills, and the like. These provide a reliable income stream with defined payment dates and amounts. Fixed-income securities are issued by governments and corporations, entities that rarely default.

On the equity side, CEFs contain most of the more dependable dividend payers, in a wide array of sectors and geographic regions. By design, they distribute 95 percent of their income to shareholders—unlike the meager income you see if you own individual stocks, even more than top-shelf "dividend" stocks.

The purpose of IFRI investing is the constant growth of both portfolio income and working capital. Even though market value isn't our primary focus, CEFs' values generally track stock market and interest-rate expectations. A rising tide lifts all ships, and vice versa.

How can you get the most total spending money? It all starts with growing your base income.

WHAT IS BASE INCOME?

"I'll bite—what's base income?" Jean said.

It's the dividends, interest, and other payouts you get from your portfolio, I explained. Most investors automatically DRIP this base income back into the same securities, instead of using it to further diversify their portfolios, so it's not something you learn to think about. That stops now.

You'll grow to love base income: It's fairly stable, even if the underlying share price of a security goes up or down. As we've discussed, issuing companies are loath to cut their dividends. With bonds, the yield is determined at purchase, so any price changes later don't affect income. CEF managers are equally reluctant to reduce their distributions.

My primary focus is to generate as much base income as possible and to keep it growing. But that's only half the income story.

WHAT ARE CAPITAL GAINS?

Capital gains are the accelerant that makes your base income grow the fastest. When you take a profit, you create additional capital. In the 2021 rally, capital gains nearly equaled the amount of base income my clients earned. Instead of the normal 8 percent in realized income, they realized around 15 percent, thanks to capital gains.

Jean cut in. "We've experienced capital gains," she said. "To pay for that trip, we sold some stock that had appreciated."

I nodded. "Investors like me call those *realized capital gains*," I said.

When the Cranes looked a little fuzzy on this, I added: When a stock's price rises above the price you paid, you have *potential* gains—but they're unrealized until you sell. They're just paper profits. Even the IRS doesn't tax us on unrealized gains . . . not yet at least.

When you sell a security at a higher price, you have realized capital gains. Realized gains are taxable in non-IRA portfolios, but there are worse things than paying taxes on realized gains. Watching them disappear in the next correction, for one.

Avoiding capital gains to reduce income taxes is one of the biggest mistakes people make. It's like walking into the boss' office and demanding a cut in pay, because you fear the increased taxes.

Here's a quick formula for calculating realized capital gains:

NET SALE PROCEEDS - COST BASIS - SELLING COSTS
= REALIZED CAPITAL GAIN (OR LOSS)

Obviously, it's preferable to generate more base income than to sell securities to get cash. If you spend the entire proceeds of a stock sale, you're reducing working capital in the process.

Now, you have a smaller portfolio with which to try to generate base income! When you need to grow spending money, that's not good.

Here's the simple formula for calculating your actual spending money:

TOTAL CASH INCOME + NET REALIZED CAPITAL GAINS - EXPENSES = TOTAL SPENDING MONEY

Over time, you want that first figure to grow. You want to pay all your expenses from base income and build your portfolio working capital with the excess income and capital gains.

WORKING CAPITAL AND LIQUIDITY: KEYS TO INCOME GROWTH

Hopefully, you remember working capital from our chat on the trip, I said. Working capital is the total of all the money you've paid to purchase your securities, plus any cash in the portfolio. Base income and realized capital gains increase your working capital, even after taxes.

To make best use of working capital and grow base income, you need to focus on investments that are always liquid and generate stable cash flow.

John shot me a quizzical look. "What do you mean by liquidity?" he said. "I think of it as how much of my portfolio I have in cash or money market accounts."

Glad you brought that up, I said. Although true, that's not what I mean—and I don't leave much cash sitting around. For our purposes, liquidity is how easy or hard it is to immediately buy or sell a security.

If you want to add a new position, can you buy it right now? If you want to take a profit on a position, is a buyer always available?

"Okay," Jean said. "If you can easily sell a security, I can see how that's basically as good as cash."

Liquidity in a security is affected by "float"—the number of shares outstanding, I added. It's illiquid if only a few shares trade daily, while many shares trading daily signals good liquidity.

Liquidity is rare in most income-purpose securities, such as debt and real estate. Only preferred stocks are moderately liquid. By placing normally illiquid securities inside CEFs, you make them completely liquid, and that's a really big deal.

Jean adds: "So no more markups to worry about or waiting weeks to unload a bond? Wow!"

DISTRIBUTIONS

How does your base income grow? Each month or quarter, each CEF you own pays your share of the income that the fund generated. These payments are known as distributions.

There can be several types of payments inside these distributions, especially in equity CEFs, so let's break them down. Distributions may include:

- **DIVIDENDS** from equities and preferred stocks
- **INTEREST** from bonds and other fixed-income securities
- **NET REALIZED CAPITAL GAINS** from profitably selling securities
- **RETURN OF CAPITAL (ROC)** from everything else

At the end of each year, your brokerage firm deducts the ROC from the cost basis of every CEF that distributed it.

That means your cost basis for those securities is now lower, and your yield just went up. Nothing wrong with that! Plus, you have additional cash to reinvest. At year-end, you may also get a special distribution, if there are profits that weren't distributed earlier.

The only way that ROC doesn't help you grow both capital and future income is if you spend all your distributions, instead of reinvesting a good portion of them.

For an example of stable CEF distributions, refer to the following chart for the PIMCO Corporate & Income Strategy Fund (PCN). It's produced very stable distributions, along with occasional special distributions, in good times and bad:

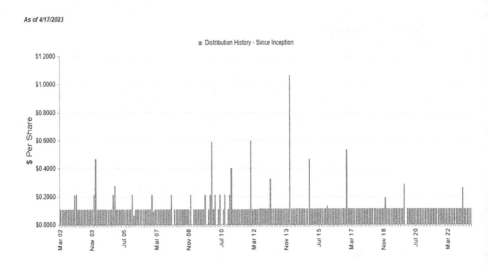

As I write this in early 2023, PCN is probably buying previously issued bonds at a discount, planning to reap capital gains in the future, when interest rates stabilize or fall. Meanwhile, shareholders enjoy reliable payouts. At its price when this picture was taken, the distribution yield was around 10 percent, from a portfolio containing over 400 individual bonds.

Before we leave this topic, let's dig a little deeper into distributions—particularly the special distributions shown as spikes in the chart above.

DISTRIBUTION DECLARATION, RECORD, AND 'EX' DATES

Just like common stocks, CEFs will periodically announce or "declare" the distributions they plan to pay. This is known as the *declaration date*. The per share amount of the distribution will be factored into the market price of the security on the declaration date.

The announcement will also set a *record date*. All shareholders on that date are entitled to receive the distribution. There's usually sometime between the declaration date and the record date. With some CEFs, future distributions are declared months in advance.

The day before the record date is called the *ex-dividend date*. As of this date, anyone who buys the CEF *isn't* entitled to the next distribution.

Note that the fund's price will fall by the amount of the distribution on the ex-date. This creates interesting possibilities for those of us who trade often and focus on profit-taking.

If you sell a CEF just before its ex-date at a profit that's greater than the distribution, you increase your velocity of money. A lot of professional traders buy just before the ex-date, particularly with larger quarterly distributions. They're in effect "buying the dividend" with a much shorter holding period.

After the ex-date, you can often buy that CEF again at a reduced price. You've profited from the excitement around the distribution and may later lock in that CEF again at a lower cost per share.

All these dates are provided in most security quote screens provided by your brokerage firm. This is not unique to CEFs, by the way—all stocks and ETFs have the same system of declaration, record, and ex-dates.

"Very interesting," Jean said. "But let's back up a bit. What makes up the ROC you mentioned earlier? What *is* 'everything else?'"

Great question—return of capital upsets some investors who don't really understand it. Let's look at this part of distributions more closely.

WHAT IS ROC?

Here's a simple definition of ROC that I like:

> *Return of capital is any portion of a CEF distribution that does not come from dividends, interest, or net realized capital gains.*

Not all CEFs include ROC in their distributions. You rarely see it in tax-free CEFs or in most taxable-income funds. Most often, it shows up in equity CEFs.

Some investors think ROC means the CEF gives back some of your original investment money. Most often, it's not that at all but payouts from the fund managers' varied investment activities.

ROC can include:

- premiums from options trading and other investing strategies
- payouts from pass-through entities, such as royalty trusts
- principal from called bonds
- ROC from other CEFs in the fund
- distributions from MLPs
- unrealized capital gains
- mortgage principal
- short-term loan repayments

There's one other reason for ROC. It stems from the fact that CEF managers like to keep payouts stable. They know retirees love reliable income.

Sometimes, if they expect to sell securities later in the year that will produce capital gains, they give shareholders an advance on that future payout. It usually all comes out even at year-end.

Critics of ROC say it over-inflates your income total, which is partially true. But it's not treated as income—and notably, it's not taxable. ROC reduces your cost basis and makes new cash available for reinvesting.

Less than one-third of CEFs even pay ROC, and the amount is usually small. I don't think ROC is a problem—I consider it a benefit. I get to reinvest that money and further diversify my portfolio.

IS ROC DESTRUCTIVE?

Some investors worry that the cash paid out in ROC reduces the CEF's investment portfolio, and so it may reduce (or "destroy") some of the fund's net asset value. ROC is no more destructive in CEFs than it is in annuities or mortgages. Both those repay principal—that's ROC.

There are certainly instances when ROC may cause a reduction in NAV. But both NAV and market value vary daily, anyway. Since ROC reduces our cost basis dollar-for-dollar, in one way, it's even better than income. It's not taxable, and you get to reinvest it immediately.

Remember, we're not concerned if securities sell at a premium or discount to NAV. So long as you don't spend the ROC, any negative impact on the CEF's NAV doesn't affect your portfolio's income productivity or working capital. This is one of the reasons why you want to limit your spending to less than 70 percent of your annual base income.

As long as your CEFs pay enough income, and you have cash to pay bills and reinvest, just keep calm and carry on, as the British say.

Let me tell you a story of how foolish it is to worry about NAV and market value:

My Aunt Alice was always my favorite. When she retired, she asked me to invest her six-figure retirement portfolio. She told me she didn't want to take any risks.

I put all her money into federally insured Ginnie Mae Trust securities (GNMAs), which contain primarily home mortgages. The yield was more than 10 percent—more than she needed for her monthly expenses.

When interest rates went up, the market value of the GNMAs went down. Alice was horrified. "I'm losing money!"

she exclaimed, even though we'd sold nothing. No losses had occurred, and bills were being paid as usual.

To my dismay, she visited a banker and took his advice to move into a ladder of "'much safer" CDs paying less than 7 percent. She was happy—until she realized her portfolio didn't generate enough cash to pay the bills!

To get enough spending money, she had to sell CDs and take early cash-out penalties. If she'd stayed focused on income, she'd have been fine.

"You know, that story actually makes me feel a little better," said Jean. "I'm struggling to let go of the 'market value' focus. But your aunt's experience shows how the income focus is smarter."

Glad to hear it, I said.

"Tell me a bit more about distributions," she added. "When do they happen, and what do you do with them?"

D-DAYS

I call the days when distributions are received, D-Days. That's because they're big days for action on my calendar. Days for decision-making.

You're getting cash, and you need to be ready to reinvest it right away. You don't want to let it sit—every day it's not invested, you don't earn any income from it.

I make it a rule to immediately reinvest distributions. That way, you never fall into the trap of thinking about market timing.

Here's another of my rules for reinvesting: At least 30 percent of distributions should be reinvested, along with all your capital gains. If you don't need all the remaining 70 percent for bills, reinvest more.

101

When do D-Days happen? The majority of CEFs make distributions on the first or last day of the month. A smaller number of payouts come mid-month and a few days before month-end.

If these dates fall on a weekend, reinvest first thing Monday. When I travel, I make sure I'm not on a plane on the first or last day of a month. I want to grab those distributions the minute they land and reinvest them.

Most portfolios don't generate large enough amounts to start new positions, so adding to existing positions that are down in price is generally the first thing I do. But larger portfolios, particularly at year's end, may generate enough to add a new position to the portfolio.

Quick reinvesting means you take full advantage of the magic of compound earnings.

COMPOUND EARNINGS

You probably remember your first savings account. It paid a little interest, then the next month, it paid a little *more*, as the interest was calculated on a slightly larger balance.

This is the beauty of compounding. The only problem is that your savings account probably paid a very low interest rate.

With CEFs, you should always see healthy yields of 6 percent or more. Reinvest the monthly distributions immediately, and your earnings compound much faster than if you receive quarterly dividends on individual stocks or semi-annual interest on bonds. CEFs may contain these securities, but their commitment to regular distributions gets you more cash to reinvest sooner.

In other words, *CEFs accelerate the compounding.*

"That makes sense," said John. "But is this reinvesting and compounding enough to cover the 4 percent withdrawals they say you should take in retirement?"

Glad you asked, I said—because that 4 percent spending rule is a pet peeve of mine.

THE 4% RETIREMENT SPENDING GUIDELINE

You hear that 4 percent rule everywhere. "You can figure 4 percent as a good estimate of how much you'll need to withdraw annually from your portfolio in retirement," your financial advisor will tell you.

This "rule" was developed in the 1990s, and it's a realistic plan of attack for establishing our withdrawal goals. In rising markets, you certainly will be able to grow your market value. But unless you take profits, no new income will be created.

In declining markets, however, withdrawals must come from selling shares, which reduces portfolio income. Long corrections can substantially deplete capital and income, particularly if there are financial emergencies.

People who spout the 4 percent rule are the same ones who DRIP distributions back into your existing securities. That means there's *no* remaining cash to spend, and you always have to sell something to cover expenses.

So, the 4 percent rule is an excellent plan, but the implementation strategy doesn't work well in the real world.

Also, most retirees could use more than 4 percent, at least some of the time. When CEFs yield 7 percent or more, it's no problem if you need a bit extra. Your distributions should more than cover your needs, while you retain all your principal and don't have to sell any-thing for spending money.

AN EXAMPLE OF INCOME GROWTH IN A CEF PORTFOLIO

Now that you understand the basics of income production, let's look (with his permission) at one of my client's IRA. I helped him switch from owning individual stocks to CEFs. By 2019, he was fully invested in CEFs.

Take a look at what happened:

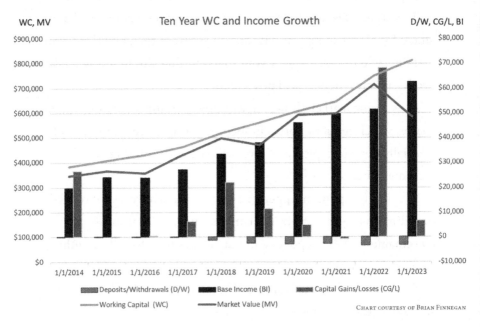

CHART COURTESY OF BRIAN FINNEGAN

This IRA had no deposits and minimal withdrawals for the 10-year period through year-end 2022—a significant down year in the stock market. What happened? When he switched to CEFs, his income and working capital grew dramatically.

He saw over 11 percent annual growth in working capital, and his base income rose over 9 percent annually. The portfolio generated an average of $52,000 per year in total income.

In 2022, despite the stock market correction, his base income was over 8 percent!

To sum up, when this client switched from individual stocks to CEFs, his working capital and income took off.

Base income tripled from less than $20,000 in 2013 to over $62,000 in 2022.

Total working capital more than doubled, from roughly $384,000 to about $812,000.

Both gained more than 10 percent per year. For comparison, growth in the S&P 500 for this period was under 11 percent, including income of under 2 percent annually.

GUIDELINES FOR GROWING INCOME

To wrap this up, let's recap my income-generation guidelines:

- **THE MOST IMPORTANT RULE: REINVEST AT LEAST 30 PERCENT OF YOUR BASE INCOME.** The more, the better.
- **IMMEDIATELY AND SELECTIVELY REINVEST DISTRIBUTIONS.** Don't DRIP, and don't try to time the market.

- **HAVE INCOME-FOCUSED PURCHASE TARGETS.** Your target will change based on market conditions—in 2023, mine was 7 percent for income-purpose funds, and at least 6 percent for equity or growth funds.
- **CHANGES IN THE MARKET VALUE—OR NAV—OF INVESTMENT-GRADE, FIXED-INCOME SECURITIES DON'T MATTER.** As long as your yield is strong, keep raking in the income.
- **HIGHER INTEREST RATES ARE THE FIXED-INCOME INVESTOR'S BEST FRIEND.** They produce more spending money and lower purchase prices. This brings opportunities to invest at a better yield or to add to existing positions and lower their cost basis.
- **LOWER INTEREST RATES ARE *ALSO* THE FIXED-INCOME INVESTOR'S BEST FRIEND.** They result in higher market values and the opportunity for profit-taking to increase working capital.

"That's really a mind blower, that interest rates going up *or* down is fine, under this system," John said.

Remember our definition of IFRI, I reminded him: *Neither interest-rate changes nor market movements should stand in the way of growing your income. Both can be used to your advantage.*

And that's a perfect segue into learning more about the next principle: profit-taking.

TEN: Principle 4: Profit-Taking

Why and When You Should Do It

THIS IS WHERE my investing approach radically diverges from the traditional buy-and-hold model you've used all your lives, I told the Cranes. I don't buy-and-hold anything. Instead, I regularly sell securities that have appreciated in value and reinvest those profits—the quicker, the better.

Why? Well, there are only three ways to get more working capital you can use to generate more spending money:

1. **DEPOSITING MORE MONEY:** Great idea, but most retirees don't have any to spare!

2. **BASE INCOME FROM INVESTMENTS:** Take those monthly distributions and reinvest.

3. **PROFIT-TAKING:** Find securities in your portfolio that have appreciated in value and sell.

Because we're on a mission to grow income, profit-taking has to be one of the strategies we use. Otherwise, income growth will be much slower.

"This is the part that feels scary," Jean said. "I mean, I don't feel like I know enough to know what to sell or when. And I want to be out enjoying my life. I don't want to start a new career as a day trader."

Don't worry, I said. That's not how I do profit-taking. I have some simple principles for knowing when and what to sell. Day trading is a whole 'other animal that can be highly speculative.

Before I get into the rules, though, I want to explain why profit-taking is such a powerful strategy for growing income. You need to understand how it accelerates your income.

MISSING THE MOMENT

To start off, let's think about what happens to your portfolio as a buy-and-hold investor. The stock market goes up-up-up, as it recently did for about a decade, until the pandemic hit. You held on that whole time, as stock values skyrocketed.

Then, the inevitable correction came. But it didn't last long, and big green numbers soon returned. After that big sigh of relief, rising interest rates tanked the market, making 2022 one of the biggest market value "down" years in history.

Did you lock in any of those huge gains, from the big run-up? No. All that happened is that your portfolio is now worth a whole lot less. You took no profits and had a painful year as you watched paper profits vanish.

This is why profit-taking matters: You shouldn't leave any winnings on the table. You should always rake in some profits along the way. Sell some now, lock in some gains, and you won't be kicking yourself the next time the market heads down.

THE POWER OF REINVESTED CAPITAL GAINS

We've talked about capital gains in our income discussion but not about the power they have to accelerate your income growth. To understand why profit-taking is a key part of my approach, let's do a little quick math:

> *Say your CEFs are yielding an average of 6 percent in base income. If you sit on what you have, you'll continue to get—and hopefully, reinvest much of—6 percent a year.*
>
> *But what if you spot a couple of securities you hold that now trade 10 percent higher than when you bought them? If you sell them, you have an immediate 10 percent profit.*

That's 4 percent more than a year's income. And you can reinvest it right now, plus any distributions already earned. A portion of this additional gain could also be used for more spending money if you need it. This may not sound like a lot, but trust me, these incremental profits add up fast.

Profit-taking speeds up compounding.

Finally, you're not at risk that this equity will lose value and you'll miss the profit opportunity—you've locked in a profit by selling. That risk is gone.

See the difference? Profit-taking is a powerful risk-mitigation strategy that also gives you more working capital, faster. It's that simple.

"This feels counterintuitive to what you told us about not liquidating assets to pay for things," John said. "What's different about this?"

I'm not cashing out these equities to spend the money, I replied. I'm immediately reinvesting it, in something with an excellent yield right now. Hopefully, it also offers more appreciation opportunities down the road.

Taking profits always does something magical: It accelerates the rate at which you grow your working capital and income. I call this effect increasing the velocity of money.

THE VELOCITY OF MONEY

The idea behind the velocity of money is that you can get more than just the regular distribution income on your CEF investments. While base income delivers steadily during the year, capital gains provide even more income, instantly.

Why? Because the faster your working capital increases, the more income you generate, and the more additional profit-taking opportunities you create.

Profit-taking increases total income while speeding up the compounding of distribution income, thus increasing the velocity of your invested capital growth.

"That sounds great!" said Jean. "How does it work?"

Let me explain:

> Say you buy 400 shares of a CEF for $10 apiece, or $4,000 total. Over the next few months, the stock's price increases by 5 percent. It's still yielding 8 percent, and you've received three monthly distributions totaling about $110.
>
> If you sell now, you'll get another $200 immediately. Total income is $310 over three months. That's a 7.75 percent gain, which translates into an annualized yield on your investment of 30 percent.
>
> You now have more than $4,310 to reinvest in new positions or add to any existing holdings that are now priced lower than you originally paid. That reduces their cost per share and increases their yield.

Jean and John looked at each other. "Wow," they said in unison.

You can never achieve this velocity-of-money effect without taking profits, I pointed out. If you buy-and-hold forever, your working capital stays locked up in the securities you bought at the start. That means most of your capital is tied up, and you have little available for new opportunities.

John seemed to follow my argument. "I get you," he said. "It sounds like you're targeting profits, not timing the market. I can see how this would work to help grow income."

There's more good news on profit-taking, I said. Technology has evolved to make it even easier to find profit opportunities.

PURCHASE OR TAX-LOT SUPERCHARGER

We've talked about how you might buy CEFs because of their generous yields. Then later, when the market value declines, you strategically buy additional shares at a lower price. Let's say they keep going down, and you do this three different times.

These second and third purchases—known as "averaging down"—lower your cost basis for this CEF and increase the yield, which is great. It also means you now have four different purchase or tax lots of that security, all at different prices. This happens often when you're an active investor and profit-taker.

Next, the market value of this CEF goes up again. The tax lot you bought at the lowest price is now up substantially. The other tax lots, not so much.

Your broker's investment software should track each tax lot separately, allowing you to easily sell just the shares that have appreciated the most. This is a great innovation that helps increase working capital while it provides more cash for productive reinvestment.

With this tax-lot level information, you can sell just your lowest-priced lot, while keeping the other lots you bought at higher prices.

Before, after waiting longer, you'd often sell your whole position at a much lower total average profit.

This way, you can stay invested in the CEF with your higher-priced tax lots. You keep getting the solid yield it offers—and wait for the value to rise more—to take profits on the pricier lots. FYI, this approach was originally developed by Scott Phillips and Bryan Finnegan, members of The Income Coach Facebook Group.

Just a tip: Make sure any broker you use can see your tax lots separately, so you can do this pinpointed profit trimming. It can be done in all types of portfolios—taxable and tax-deferred. Some brokerage firms may say it can't be done in qualified (non-taxable) accounts because it doesn't matter tax wise. I say that it's even more important in such portfolios because no taxes means even faster income growth!

A RECIPE FOR GROWING RETIREMENT INCOME — FASTER

I had one last point to make about profit-taking.

On our trip, we talked about minimizing risk and how important it is for retirees, I said. The four principles I've just taught you are what I call the four great risk minimizers. Together, they're like a recipe for investment success:

QDI + PT = SAFELY MAXIMIZED INCOME WITH MINIMIZED RISK

Quality securities, Diversified portfolios, a focus on Income production, plus Profit-Taking. That's the recipe for achieving the most income with your portfolio, without taking too much risk.

I use this formula when I create lists of acceptable securities for my own investing. They're the rules I use to create my "selection universes" for CEF investing.

MY FLEXIBLE RULE FOR PROFIT-TAKING

"So how do you know when it's time to sell?" asked Jean. "You said you were selling when values went up 'substantially'—how big of a profit should there be, to make it worth selling this CEF and reinvesting, instead of just keeping it?"

Great question! I have a set of what I think of as flexible formulae for deciding when it's time to sell a CEF. I say "flexible" because all the rules may not apply in every situation.

The rule: No profit over 5 percent should be left unrealized, except in three circumstances:

1. The profit is less than a known, upcoming special distribution.
2. There are more than two to four positions you hold with profits over 5 percent depending on portfolio size. I don't advise selling too many positions at once, so in this scenario, some will wait.
3. If the yield on money market funds is higher than the anticipated profit, you can sell more positions than when it is not.

The inflexible part of the rule: Profit-taking is never about market timing.

I never second-guess a profit-taking decision and think, "Maybe it'll go up more." If it's gone up over 5 percent, it's time to take at least some profits on this security now. If it's a large position, and new high-yield purchase opportunities are few, you may want to sell just the most profitable lots.

THE COST OF FREQUENT TRADING

Now, if you're our age, you might worry about all the fees you'd rack up, trading in and out of these positions.

"I did wonder about that," Jean said.

Here's the good news—the internet is your friend here. Since the rise of online, self-managed accounts at Schwab, Fidelity, and the like, the cost of trades has been driven down to near zero! Brokers usually don't charge a fee for executing trades these days, either. Your financial professional is paid a salary by their company or sometimes a retainer fee by you.

In the past, I would have looked harder at the percentage gain, to make sure I would still see a profit after fees. But that's all gone now. You're free to buy and sell as often as you like without racking up any per-trade fees.

"I didn't realize that" Jean said. "Thanks for clarifying!'

"What about the capital gains tax?" asked John. "Doesn't the tax bite make it not worthwhile to sell?"

It doesn't, I said. Let me explain why.

TAXES AND PROFIT-TAKING: DON'T LET THE TAIL WAG THE DOG

Here's the thing about profits: There is no such thing as a bad profit.

As I said earlier, if your boss offers you a $10,000-a-year raise, you don't turn it down because you'll have to pay more in taxes.

Maybe at your tax rate, that'll be a net $7,500 more, or even less. But I've no doubt you'll take that money with a big smile.

Profit-taking by selling securities isn't really any different. You'd never turn down more salary, which is taxed—so why turn down profits that trigger capital-gains tax? That's letting the tail wag the dog.

If you're really unhappy about capital-gains tax, you can always focus on securities you've held longer than one year and take long-term capital gains instead of short-term ones. Our tax system is set up to motivate you to hold equities longer, so long-term capital gains have a lower tax rate. But you'd be amazed at how often short-term gains disappear before they become long.

Here's an example: In the '80s, T. Boone Pickens was leading hostile takeovers in the oil industry. The gains were incredible in several different holdings, and the whole sector was way up in price. One of my clients, who was 15 percent invested in this sector, instructed me not to take profits until after January 1, to push the taxes into the next year. The takeovers ceased, the sector went back to normal, and by January there were no profits left.

Remember: A day without profits is like a fine meal without wine.

Think about how stocks like Netflix and Peloton boomed at the beginning of the pandemic, only to come crashing back to Earth once vaccinations arrived and most people resumed their busy lives. If I'd owned those individual stocks, I would have sold my shares in those positions on the way up and locked in the profits, long before the crash, which is what I did in the CEFs that contained them.

Meanwhile, buy-and-hold investors never profited from that spectacular run-up.

DON'T TAKE LOSSES TO OFFSET GAINS

Some people solve their unhappiness with paying capital-gains taxes by taking tax losses to offset the gains. I think it's an ill-advised strategy, which is often referred to euphemistically by professionals as tax-loss harvesting.

That goes double if you have plans to buy back that equity soon. If you buy it back within 30 days, the loss isn't deductible and you haven't offset the gain after all.

Think of it in terms of working capital. Say I sell a stock for a $1,000 loss to offset one I sold for a $1,000 profit. If you're in a 35 percent tax bracket, you just saved $350 in taxes—but you lost $1,000 of working capital.

That's not smart—unless it's some leftover, lower-quality security, or a really low-yield position.

Some people sell perfectly good securities—ones still producing more than 6 percent income—to offset capital gains. That makes no financial sense.

Also, don't forget that distributions are taxable, too, if they're in a taxable account. You're paying taxes anyway—on salary, on taxable distributions and, yes, on capital gains. Often, the capital-gains tax is at a lower rate than the others.

Stay focused on what matters: the velocity of money and finding opportunities to supercharge it.

REINVESTING PROFITS

When you learned about base income, you learned to reinvest those distributions into more high-quality CEFs with strong yields. You should do the same thing with your profit-taking cash.

Think of your qualified, diversified universe of CEFs as a desktop full of 8 percent yield buttons you can push to invest in another CEF. If I have enough cash from taking profits—say, over $5,000—maybe I'll buy a whole new position or two. If it's less, I might buy one new position and average down on an existing holding. There are many options.

Just don't forget to watch your diversification mix, and not let any one security even approach 5 percent of your total portfolio.

"One last question about this," John said. "How do you know what the market's going to do, so you know if it's a good time to take a lot of profits or not?"

The short answer is nobody knows. But we do know that markets always cycle up and down—and you need to manage your portfolio based on where we are in the cycle. That means understanding market cycles—and that's the next principle to learn about.

ELEVEN: Principle 5: Understanding Market Cycles

What They Are and How to Manage Them

F ROM OUR DISCUSSIONS—AND just because you're lived long enough—you probably know that stock market averages and interest rates cycle up and down over time, I told the Cranes. Like Mother Nature with the seasons, there is a natural ebb and flow.

No market rally lasts forever. At some point, values come back down and align more closely with the intrinsic value of the underlying securities. In the same way, a deep correction will eventually turn upward again as news gets better, economies improve, or politics get less scary. There's never a precise reason, always a combination of things that change market direction.

Buy-and-hold investors live in fear of market corrections or interest-rate hikes that might negatively impact their securities' market value. By contrast, income-focused retirement investors like me accept and expect cycles as the natural order of things—and manage our portfolios to take advantage of whatever is happening.

We know we can't predict the future. What we can do is apply our risk-minimization strategies to current market trends. There's no need to worry, because there is always an opportunity to grow income, whichever way things are trending. It's all in understanding how to manage your portfolio and alter your strategy, depending on where we are in the market cycle.

MARKET CYCLE INVESTMENT MANAGEMENT

In the 1970's, I developed a process of aligning income-focused investment strategies with current market conditions that I dubbed Market Cycle Investment Management. MCIM recognizes the cyclical nature of markets, sectors, interest rates, and economies, and tries to prepare for and take advantage of market value movements in either direction.

The strategies that accomplish this are ones you've already learned—targeted profit-taking and diversifying your investments across the three types of CEFs: taxable-income, tax-free, and equity/ growth purpose.

Always remember that market value is a secondary concern for us. If you're getting the yield you need in current holdings, you can continue to follow your QDI+PT principles. Keep collecting your distributions and reinvesting that income in CEFs with favorable current yields. Gradually sell your most profitable positions as their market value gains approach 5 percent, then reinvest. Same old-same old.

It's notable that an income-focused investor with diversified CEFs generating strong distributions may not need to make many changes when markets rise or fall. You'll see TV pundits in hysterics when markets make sudden moves. Your job is to stay calm and analyze the situation.

Note that even at the top of the market in late 2021, CEFs in my selection universe remained at yields averaging well above 7 percent for taxable-income and equity funds, and around 5 percent for tax-free CEFs. Remember the chart of how the CEF PCN continued to issue near-identical distributions through cycles of rallies and corrections:

As of 4/17/2023

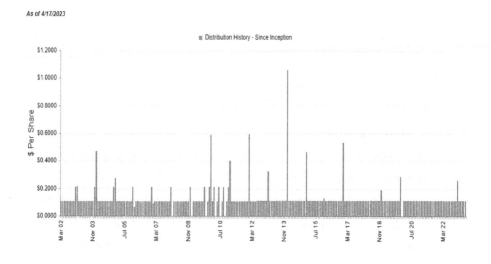

This chart reminds us that up- or down-market movements typically have no impact on either working capital or income production.

That said, market conditions *do* present income-focused investors with some unique opportunities to grow income, in both the "up" and "down" parts of the cycle. It's important to know how to tweak the system to reap additional benefits when market values see a prolonged rise or fall. Let's discuss those opposite market conditions one at a time and talk about how to adapt.

INVESTING DURING A RALLY

It's always abundantly clear when rallies are in progress. Choose your favorite stock market chart website for the S&P 500 or the bond markets, then set it to show five years of data. You can also look at individual CEF price trends on CEF Connect to analyze price vs. NAV trends over extended time periods. The trend line will be obvious.

Unlike traditional investing programs—in which you'd watch markets soar, take no action, and watch your paper profits vanish in the next correction—my approach sees the rally as a major profit-taking opportunity.

During an extended rally, you can often take profits higher than my usual 5 percent target. The market value of many older securities will soar higher than your cost basis.

But it would be foolish to sell dozens of positions at once. In these rare circumstances, ratcheting the sell target to 6 to 7 percent can be a good, but temporary, strategy. Even if you're not watching your portfolio daily, make arrangements to never leave a 7 percent gain or a $1,000 profit go unrealized.

Yes, I said *never*. It's far better to have the inconvenience of too much money left to reinvest than to have left profits on the table to vanish in a sudden downturn.

During many past rallies, I saw how one or more stocks would make a huge gain based on a takeover story or for some other sector-related reason. We used to call these events "sell all profits"—a very exciting call indeed. Sometimes hundreds of positions would be sold for as many portfolios, all at significant profits. Absolutely never say no to a major profit, regardless of the circumstances.

Never take the chance of losing the profit entirely. Go ahead and sell— at least the most profitable lot within a position—even if values are so high that you have to reinvest at yields a point or so below your norm. Just buy fewer shares.

Too much uninvested cash that must wait for a reasonable yield beats the alternative. It's not ideal, but it's not as bad as that sinking feeling you get when a stock market crash erases all your paper profits. And with hundreds of suitable CEFs to choose from, you'll rarely have to sit on cash.

Profits always increase working capital, and more working capital will eventually produce more income.

TIPS FOR INVESTING IN A RALLY

As securities' prices rise, these are things to consider and/or actions to take:

- **AT ALL-TIME MARKET HIGHS (ATHS), ALWAYS TAKE A FEW EXTRA PROFITS, JUST BECAUSE.** Take profits on the largest-percentage gainers. If any are over 5 percent, you might sell positions more than once per day, just in case the rally ends tomorrow. Yes, you may have uninvested cash as a result—and that's okay for now.

- **SMALLER INITIAL POSITIONS INCREASE DIVERSIFICATION AND FACILITATE FUTURE ADDITIONS.** As prices move higher, initial positions taken in new securities should be up to 50 percent smaller than usual. If you usually put $4,000 into a new position, you might go down to $3,000 or lower. You'll end up with more than the usual number of securities in your portfolio, but it's essential to take small positions now to leave "room" to add lower-cost shares in the next correction without any position exceeding 5 percent of working capital.

- **RE-EXAMINE YIELDS IN LARGE POSITIONS BY PURCHASE LOT.** Over the years, some positions will grow uncomfortably large. Even if they continue to produce good distributions, some shares could be sold to better diversify.

- **PRUNE SOME WEAKER POSITIONS.** At market ATHs, analyze your largest few positions—or any securities that represent over 4 percent of working capital or $15,000. If there are no recent lot profits, look for any older "lots" that now yield less than 5 percent. These lots may be pruned from the positions, even at a loss—and moved into higher-yielding opportunities. But don't get carried away—limit total portfolio losses to 1 percent of working capital per year.

- **DON'T INCREASE YOUR COST BASIS.** Never buy shares at a price above your existing cost basis. That would increase your average cost per share and lower your yield on that security. This is a major "never do," which is often violated by using automatic reinvesting programs, such as dollar-cost averaging and DRIPs.

- **SELL ON GOOD NEWS.** If a CEF shoots up in price, look for the news before pulling the sell trigger. There may be a special distribution announcement, where the distribution is bigger than the profit. If a large special distribution is involved, remember to sell for as little as 80 percent of the special distribution before the ex-dividend date.

- **REMEMBER, THE LONGER THEY LAST, THE RISKIER RALLIES BECOME.** There's more risk in a rally—more so than in a correction— because we know values will fall back to supported levels eventually. That's why you lock in profits while they're attainable, especially if there are still buying opportunities in your selection universe.

- **KEEP THE MARKET CYCLE IN MIND.** Remember, no rally will last forever. Don't become a speculator who ignores the nature of markets and starts to believe the market will go up forever. Always take your target profits—almost without exception.

"So, in a rally, there's more profit-taking opportunity," John said. "I get that. And if you need to wait a bit to reinvest, so be it."

Correct, I said, but rarely is reinvestment a problem. You'll be surprised at how readily you'll find CEFs that meet our requirements. Remember that markets don't move in a straight line up or down. In a rally, there will still be some downward movements to take advantage of.

In any case, remember:

There's no such thing as a bad profit, and never look back after taking one!

"What about in the opposite situation?" Jean asked. "When the market is crashing, we know there are lots of opportunities to invest at good values. It's 'buy low' time. But how do you find any profits to take so you have the money to invest?"

INVESTING DURING A CORRECTION

When we enter the "down" phase of the market cycle, profits at our 5 percent "must sell" target level pretty much disappear, I replied. But I'll usually still do some selling. You take whatever you can get, because of the tremendous income-growth opportunities that corrections provide.

In this scenario, think of any profit as more a reallocation of assets that creates a more potent income stream. You can buy at lower prices now, which reduces your overall cost basis and gives you higher-yield positions.

To sum up, our normal investing rules must bend during a correction. With stock prices trending downward, "any profit" might become the goal. Better to sell a position for a small profit if you can move that income into an existing CEF holding that's trading below your cost. That way, you grow the whole position's yield.

In a falling market, your CEF selection universes will be growing, because yields rise with lower market prices.

"Do you sell your whole position, if you see you're at 5 percent over your cost basis?" Jean asked.

In general, I'm a whole-position seller, I said. I've seen too many quick turnarounds in market direction to take the chance of letting them slip away. Waiting for more is one of the biggest mistakes investors make. Don't get greedy!

"But what if in a down market, none of your CEFs are up in value?" asked John. "Are there ever no profits to take?"

You'll be surprised how seldom that will be true, I said. Sure, 2022 was a lean year for profit-taking. And that will happen now and then. But remember, the markets don't travel in a straight line, up or down. There will be small rallies during an overall correction that will give you some profit-taking opportunities, particularly in recently purchased lots you added at lower prices to improve your cost basis.

If it feels like we're in a pre-rally—just starting to transition from a correction back into a rally—you still take your profits and reinvest. If you're wrong, the profit is in your pocket.

If you're right, the same forces that would raise that CEF you just sold higher will raise the replacement CEFs just as well. So it's not a big worry. You've heard the expression: "A rising tide lifts all boats."

We've all seen what traders call the "dead-cat bounce": The market goes up for a few days, people get excited that a rally is starting, but it soon settles back down where it was again. Meanwhile, you can use that short uptick to take some profits and reinvest at still-acceptable yields on CEFs that didn't bounce back as much as others.

At the bottom of a market cycle, you're lucky if you have a few securities that are up 1 percent. You'll have to decide whether to sell to take advantage of opportunities to buy new positions at low prices and lock in higher yields. Selling now creates an infusion of new capital that can be used to reduce cost basis and increase yields.

Remember that we're well diversified, holding CEFs with different types of securities inside them. If something out there is on an upswing, it's likely that we own it in one of our CEF portfolios. So long as there are profits to reap and reasonable opportunities to invest in, profit-taking stays a regular part of your activities.

Investors my age still remember October 19, 1987, one of the largest single-day crashes in history. If you learn anything from me, it should

be to never feel "wiped out" in a sudden correction again. Investors in my firm were rubbing their hands together on that day, excited by all the opportunities that massive correction created to invest at lower prices.

VISIT THE LINK ABOVE
FOR MORE ABOUT
THE '87 CRASH

Most market swings only increase or decrease market values by between 10 to 20 percent and take months to develop. But a big crash like '87 can create huge opportunities for QDI-focused investors. The COVID-19 dip in March 2020 was a similar phenomenon, but it lasted just a few months. We were all over it!

As we discuss this in spring 2023, we're 18 months into a correction in interest-rate sensitive securities and still down more than 15 percent in the market averages. That's a lot, historically speaking. Maybe this gives you a sense of the variance you're likely to see—and why I'm such a fan of taking profits when a CEF is up as little as 5 percent.

TIPS FOR INVESTING WHEN PRICES ARE DOWN

As securities' prices sink, these are things to consider and/or actions to take:

- **WHEN PRICES ARE DOWN, BUY MORE.** When market prices are falling, buy more new and existing securities. You may see CEFs trading as much as 20 percent below your cost basis and yielding upward of 8 percent. Reduce your cost basis and increase yield in existing positions. As the correction continues, use more realized capital gains and regular distributions to start new positions, in anticipation of quick turnarounds when the markets start to rally again.

- **NEVER SELL A POSITION DURING A CORRECTION DUE SOLELY TO A CONCERN ABOUT LOWER PRICES.** So long as fund distributions are stable and above minimum acceptable levels and nothing critically wrong has been reported, hang on. Selling out of fear is another major "never do" in CEF portfolios.

- **ADD PREFERRED STOCK AND CONVERTIBLE CEFS.** These two investment types tend to appreciate more quickly once a stock market rally begins.

- **CONSIDER SELLING ANYTHING ABOVE BREAKEVEN TO REINVEST FOR A LOWER-COST BASIS AND A HIGHER YIELD.** During a correction, I may call a client to explain: "I sold XYZ at breakeven to spread the proceeds among five positions in order to reduce their cost basis and increase yield." I never hesitate to make that move.

- **WHEN MARKET VALUES ARE LOW, INCOME SECURITIES' YIELDS ARE HIGH.** When you can buy any CEF, income, or equity, at the low end of its normal trading range, that's a great opportunity to lock in a high yield.

- **JUST BECAUSE THE MARKET'S LOW DOESN'T MEAN EVERYTHING IS A GOOD BUY.** Quality, diversification, and income still matter. Continue doing your homework.
- **PRIORITIZE NEW POSITIONS OVER EXISTING ONES.** During a correction, I'll add to some positions that are down 10 percent or more from my cost basis, but not less than that. I'd rather take a small, new position in a CEF for more diversity.
- **IT'S A GREAT TIME TO SWITCH INTO CEFS.** If you have a traditional investment portfolio with individual stocks, mutual funds, and/or ETFs, a correction provides a great opportunity to become an income-focused retirement investor. Many CEFs will be at the low end of their trading range and offer attractive yields.

One final idea: With all the great buying opportunities in a correction, consider putting more cash into your investment portfolios if you can.

KEEP YOUR EMOTIONS OUT OF IT

Whether the market is going up or down, one thing should be constant: Profit-taking and reinvesting decisions should not be driven by emotions.

I like to say there is no l-o-v-e in investing.

You may have loved working for the company that you accumulated thousands of shares in over the years but look at that holding critically. What's its yield? Is your portfolio not well diversified because you have a supersized block of those shares?

If so, sell 10 percent of it annually and pay the capital-gains tax, until you're done with it. Few if any common stocks compare with CEFs for yield. What you're holding isn't rational, and it isn't going to fulfill your goal of having ample retirement money to support your lifestyle. If it's a great investment, you'll find it inside several CEFs.

Try not to get emotionally attached to any security you own. These investments only exist for two reasons: to provide income to spend in retirement with as little risk as possible and to provide profits that can increase income even further.

There's no "know" in investing. We have no idea which way the market will move next, and neither does anyone else. That's why we stick to the rules I've just laid out for buying and selling under different conditions.

Remember, as income-focused investors, *we thrive on market volatility.* I often say volatility is an income investor's best friend. Without ups and downs, it would be a lot harder to take profits and find new positions with high yields!

If you keep taking profits and reinvesting, you'll do well. There is less profit-taking opportunity during a correction, and yields are lower during rallies. But if you keep following the QDI+PT principles and adapt them for current market conditions, you'll keep building total annual income in either environment.

"How do you know if all these moves are working out the way you want?" asked Jean, "Am I reaching my income-investment goals?"

That's what our final principle addresses. It's critical that you periodically take time to analyze your results and see if you need to make any changes.

TWELVE: Principle 6: Assessing Investment Performance

How to Measure Success

"**H**OW OFTEN DO you look at your performance?" asked John. "And how do you know how well your investment shopping center is doing?"

I track month-to-month income and perform quarter-to-quarter comparisons of both income and working capital growth, I replied.

But there's a caveat: While I may look at income and working capital performance through calendar time periods, that doesn't mean the calendar year has any particular importance to an income-focused retirement investor. My monthly statements provide all the needed data.

Even though you'll hear companies crow about how their stock performed this year compared to last year, IFRI investors care about constant income growth, not rising market value. So long as you're growing working capital, market value also grows when the market cycle turns upward.

Your investment shopping center helps set performance expectations. CEF investors own such a broad swath of the world economy that our portfolios follow along with what world markets are experiencing and expecting. That's what runs the market cycle and what CEFs take advantage of. It's your own personal economic indicator.

OBJECTIVE-BASED PERFORMANCE EVALUATION

When you assess portfolio performance, return to the question: Why are you investing—what's your goal? It's to generate as much income as possible, while not taking unnecessary risks.

To see if you're achieving that goal, check two important metrics:

1. Is base income growing, quarter over quarter and year over year?
2. Is working capital growing over time? If not, why not?

Growing these two figures is what matters most—because retirees need a growing money supply to keep ahead of inflation and other rising discretionary expenses.

With that in mind, I want to see base income exceed expenses and increased working capital over time. Increasing base income gives you more money to reinvest, as well as the money you need to live on. If base income and working capital aren't growing, you may need to cut back on your withdrawals to make sure you're reinvesting enough to foster growth.

With our stringent selection criteria and diversification rules, losses will rarely be a significant problem. But if you sell securities to get cash for living expenses, that could cause shrinking working capital.

The formula is simple:

$$\text{BASE INCOME} + \text{NET CAPITAL GAINS} + \text{DEPOSITS} - \text{WITHDRAWALS} = \text{IMPACT ON WORKING CAPITAL.}$$

If trading becomes negative—you're forced to sell securities at a loss—or withdrawals increase, working capital will suffer.

Less working capital growth may also be the result of a major correction—if too many CEFs are forced to cut distributions. But that has rarely happened, in my experience. Remember, reductions in market value alone have no impact on working capital.

Here's an illustration of income growth during the 2022 piece of the correction that began in fall 2021. The data is derived from my analysis of 90 different CEF portfolios with a total market value of just over $40 million.

The Equity Index Total is a composite total of the S&P 500, DJIA, and Nasdaq prices. The Dow and S&P did slightly better in '22, the Nasdaq quite a bit worse. Total index values are on the right, and EOY stands for end-of-year.

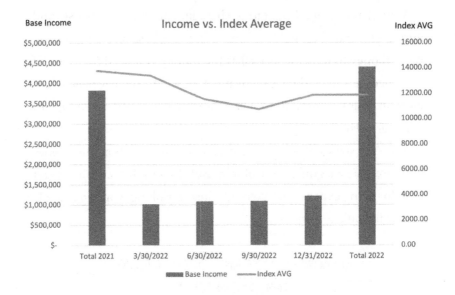

As you can see, base income rose each quarter, growing by nearly $600,000 for the year. That's more than 15 percent income growth in a correction year.

Only 10 of the accounts were as much as 50 percent invested in equities; 52 percent had none.

2 KINDS OF CAKE

With IFRI investing, I think of just two investment types: income purpose and growth purpose, with all stock CEFs on the growth side.

Imagine each investment type is a cake—the main purpose—with frosting, which is a bonus that sweetens the deal. You know, the icing on top.

With income-purpose securities, the cake is the distributions that add to your base income. That's the main reason you hold them. The frosting on this cake is capital gains that become available when the market value of these CEFs rises and you sell at a profit.

With growth-purpose securities, things work the opposite way. The cake is the capital gains you reap when these CEFs increase in market value during market upswings. It may not happen every year, but over the long term, market values of equities have always trended upward. The frosting is the generous distributions you get while owning these equity based CEFs. Typically, distributions in equity CEFs run nearly as high as the distributions for income securities, so it's some extra tasty frosting.

When you assess each of these desserts, you're looking to see if they're each doing their job. Are the income-purpose CEFs generating the income you need and expect? Are the growth securities' market value increasing? If not, is it because of overall market conditions, or is it time to reassess your positions?

WATCH THE LINES THAT MATTER

Market value investors obsess about what the market is doing. That's the only chart they pay much attention to. Is the Dow or the S&P up or down? Is my portfolio doing better than the averages?

Always remember, that's not our primary focus. We use market value in buy-and-sell decision-making and to help determine where we are in the market cycle. We know how to profit no matter what the market is doing. Instead, when I create a graph of portfolio performance, the lines I watch are:

- **BASE INCOME (DISTRIBUTIONS):** This line should move steadily upward, as you compound those distributions through reinvestment. The less you withdraw, the more quickly this line rises.
- **CUMULATIVE NET REALIZED CAPITAL GAINS:** This figure is most important to track in the first few years. Are you successfully taking profits and reinvesting when gains are available? If you're not adding to your working capital steadily through profit-taking, it may be time to tweak your profit-taking rules.
- **WORKING CAPITAL:** This line should always be moving upward. An average growth rate of 5 to 10 percent a year is a reasonable target, depending on the mix you've selected between growth- and income-purpose securities. It takes at least two years to plot your average working capital growth. You'll need that much data to determine how well your compounding and velocity growth strategies are working.

Check out this chart that compares working capital growth with S&P performance during the boom-to-bust period from year-end 2020 to the end of 2022. These figures are derived from a combined CEF portfolio of $18.7 million at year-end 2020. The asset allocation in these portfolios was roughly 35 percent equity CEFs and 65 percent income CEFs.

	EOY 2019	3/31/2020	6/30/2021	9/30/2021	12/31/2021	EOY 2022
S&P 500	3235	4020	4352	4357	4766	3840
Total WC	$18,712,479	$19,171,879	$20,147,752	$20,571,546	$21,411,510	$22,669,140

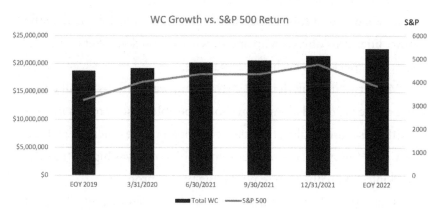

As you'd expect, working capital grew each quarter during 2021. It ended the year up roughly 14 percent. Then in 2022, as the S&P 500 fell 19 percent, these portfolios added another 7 percent to working capital, closing the two-year period up more than 21 percent—a gain of nearly $4 million.

Bottom line: This chart illustrates the true advantage of CEF-based, income-focused investing for retirement. In a very bad stock market year, the CEF portfolios kept delivering more income. Working capital increased because all the 2021 profits and most distribution income from both years was continually reinvested. Also, note that the working capital growth is after all fees and expenses.

ASSESSING TOTAL PORTFOLIO MARKET VALUE

Finally, we look at total portfolio market value over time. Unlike the other lines, this one goes up and down with stock market and interest-rate expectation cyclical fluctuations.

Market value growth is not a straight upward line, as we all know. But as the years roll along, you should be able to see growth in your portfolio's market value, thanks to continued reinvestment of realized income. However, if the market value line ever moves higher than the working capital line, you're not taking profits properly.

Reinvestment of 30 to 40 percent of base income and all capital gains is always the paved road to working capital growth and market value growth during rallies.

If your market value doesn't increase in an extended up-cycle, it may be time to review the QDI fundamentals. Make sure you're screening well—selecting securities of appropriate quality, adequate diversification, and ample income production.

If you've had more than a very few losses, the fundamentals are likely the problem.

Finally, if your assessment shows a level below reasonable expectations, one other possibility may be the mix of income- vs. growth-purpose securities. The mix is decided in the planning process called asset allocation, so let's talk about this concept next.

THIRTEEN: Asset Allocation With CEFs

YOU MIGHT THINK it's funny for me to discuss asset allocation, when I know you probably learned about it with your first
401(k) plan at work, I said.

John nodded. "Exactly right."

Back then, a financial planner probably came to your office and
did a checklist with you to determine the level of market exposure
you should have based on your age, needs, and risk tolerance. As you
got older, you adjusted the mix and got more heavily into fixed-income securities.

Once a year, you—or your broker—rebalanced the portfolio to
the desired proportions. To accomplish that, if your portfolio was too

heavy in stocks, they'd sell the worst performers, which to them meant stocks with declining market values. They would suggest taking losses, even though this would shrink your working capital.

Am I right?

"That describes it," said John. "I remember being told to be happy I had a tax write-off for the losses."

It really annoys me when I hear that. Why take losses on perfectly good securities to do something that should be dealt with more frequently?

Less working capital results in lower future base income. That's not how I manage portfolios! There are better ways to keep your portfolio in sync with your asset allocation plan. Also, you don't want to drive yourself crazy watching the markets every day and worrying if they're going down. Thankfully, income-focused retirement investing removes that worry.

The good news is that asset allocation works differently when you're not a market value focused, buy-and-hold investor. We have more flexibility to keep our allocation mix on track, with regularly reinvested distributions and capital gains.

But before I get into how I keep portfolios balanced, let's begin at the beginning—with how to set allocation goals.

PURPOSE-BASED INVESTING

IFRI investors start by thinking about the purpose of retirement investing.

Remember, you're investing your money to generate income. That means you're not too concerned about market value. And your success doesn't depend much on whether the market is going up (though, over the course of your life, it certainly should).

The aim is to grow working capital so you're always producing more income. That's your primary focus, not market value growth.

When you choose your allocation percentages, always focus on this purpose.

SAFETY FIRST

The other key factor in your asset allocation decision is to temper your quest for income with your desire to limit risk.

That's why both growth- and income-purpose CEFs containing an average of hundreds of securities are your investment vehicles of choice. We also spread our dollars among a diverse array of quality CEFs, mitigating risk even more.

With your purpose and need to limit risk in mind, we're ready to decide on your asset allocation.

INCOME BUCKET VS. GROWTH BUCKET

The big question in asset allocation is always the same: What percentage of your portfolio will be exposed to equities, and what percentage will go into fundamentally safer fixed-income securities?

Keep in mind that risk is a relative term. We don't include riskier CEFs in our selection universes right from the get-go. For asset allocation purposes, the distinction is simply between equity and debt. ABC company's debt will always be a safer investment than ABC's stock.

Here's my guideline for older investors: If you've put away money steadily for years and have a substantial retirement account, anyone in their 50s shouldn't be any more than 50 percent in the stock market. (If you're a late starter, you'll probably need a bit more stock market exposure for a while, because you need more growth.)

Maybe, if you're a more risk-averse person or your portfolio is smaller, you'll alter these percentages a bit. But that's a good starting point. As you approach retirement, I'd ordinarily recommend you be 70 percent in income CEFs and only 30 percent in growth.

Once you've chosen an asset allocation that feels good to you, you'll revisit it as you age or your circumstances change. Typically, every five years, you should adjust the stock exposure downward. You alter it a little bit, getting increasingly conservative over time. But again, this will vary with your personal circumstances and overall income status. I'm 77 years old, and I still have about 30 percent of my portfolio in equity CEFs.

MARKET TIMING ISN'T PART OF ASSET ALLOCATION

Did you ever have an investment advisor tell you that you should get more heavily into stocks because, hey, the market is going up right now? Or the inverse—you should get out of the market because the Dow is going down?

By now, I'm sure you realize that market timing doesn't work. You don't change an asset allocation plan based on current stock market trends.

In IFRI investing, you set allocation parameters based on your goals, not on fluctuating market conditions. With your income focus and CEFs as your investment vehicle, look at whether your portfolio is generating the income you want. As you've learned, your CEFs will usually keep paying similar-sized distributions, even when the market is trending downward.

FILLING THE BUCKETS

Once you've settled on your asset allocation target, you need to make investments that achieve that balance. You'll buy positions in some quality CEFs focused on equities and others in fixed-income securities, until your portfolio is allocated according to your chosen percentages. Remember, your investment decision is always based upon the amount of working capital you invest in each CEF, not their market value.

You've already learned about my QDI principles and how to create selection universes of the fundamentally best CEFs. From there, it should be easy to choose CEFs that make your investment mix fit your allocation goals. Your risk is low, investing in a broad mix of quality CEFs, so we're focused on our purpose and mitigating risk with our choices.

MANAGING THE ALLOCATION WITH EVERY INVESTMENT DECISION

Once you've set your allocations and made your initial investments, the real beauty of the IFRI investing approach becomes obvious. Where traditional buy-and-hold, market value investors rebalance annually based on market value, IFRI investors have much more flexibility to keep their allocation in balance.

"I bet I know how," said Jean. "We're getting base income throughout the month and reinvesting it right away, along with any capital gains we've had that month, right?"

Exactly, I said. Now, you don't have to wait until year-end to rebalance. You can tweak your allocation every month, if you want. You can do it at your convenience, with every reinvestment transaction.

Say you notice a position has grown to more than 5 percent of your portfolio, throwing your allocation balance out of whack. You can sell any profitable part of that position and put it in the opposite bucket. Maybe you need to put more of that month's distributions into the opposite bucket, too.

Presto! You're rebalanced. As long as you don't let any distribution cash sit around, you have the power to keep your allocation at or near your target all year long. And remember that it's a target, not an absolute. A little leeway in either direction is totally acceptable because many of our CEFs are mixed-content entities.

"I love that," said Jean.

WE'LL MEET AGAIN

It had been a long day of talking through income-focused retirement investing principles. I noticed the Cranes were checking their watches. When I asked if they needed to go, they both nodded and began gathering their things.

"We need to hit the road for home—I like to get there before dark," Jean said. "Any chance you'd consider coming to Richmond to visit? I'd love to see some examples of this system in action and learn about how you'd switch retirement accounts like ours into CEFs."

John added, "I also still have some questions I'd love to talk through with you—and to have you take a look at our portfolio."

As it happens, my son and grandson live not far from the Cranes—and Sandie and I planned to visit in December. We made a date to reconnect then and said our goodbyes.

FOURTEEN: Why CEFs Beat Mutual Funds and ETFs for Retirement Investing

VISITING FAMILY IN Richmond for the holidays is a tradition Sandie and I always look forward to. After a quick lunch stop at the outlet mall off route 95 in North Carolina, we drove north through Virginia until arriving in Richmond, passing by the charming brick facades of the historic downtown area, now adorned with a few inches of picturesque recent snow. We checked in at The Jefferson Hotel, a classic destination that we stay at frequently.

We arrived a few days ahead of our usual family visit to allow time for visiting the Cranes. Their home was just a few miles away. Sadly, no golf for this trip! My laptop was loaded up with CEF portfolio examples, ready to share.

After a good night's rest, we bundled up in our warmest coats against the Northern cold and drove out to the Cranes for brunch at their home. After we cleared our dishes, I set up my laptop. John and Jean took a seat on either side of me, while Sandie pulled out her iPad.

At this point, you know the theory behind IFRI investing, I said. Now, I'm here to show you how this approach works in real portfolios— and how it compares to traditional retirement investing.

3 WAYS TO COMPARE CEFS WITH MUTUAL FUNDS AND ETFS

Keep in mind that CEFs are pass-through trusts, I reminded the Cranes. They're required to give at least 95 percent of the income they produce to their shareholders.

Mutual funds and ETFs have no such requirement, so they don't hand out much in distributions. They assume you'll get the money you need from market value growth over time.

Individual company stocks care even less about giving you money. Could you imagine asking Amazon to send 95 percent of their profits to their common stockholders? I think you know how that would go over.

There are three important ways to compare CEFs with mutual funds and ETFs:

1. **CEFS ARE MORE FLEXIBLE THAN MUTUAL FUNDS.** CEFs trade all day, every day. By contrast, if you put in an order to buy a mutual fund, it'll be executed at the market open the next day—at whatever price that fund's value has been reset to overnight. It's harder to be precise in buying and selling.

2. **THE CONTENT IS SIMILAR.** What's contained inside CEFs, mutual funds, and ETFs is not all that different. All three vehicles usually contain hundreds of securities. Managers at each choose a focus for their fund, whether global, growth, sector-specific, fixed income, or whatever.

3. **ONLY CEFS FOCUS ON INCOME.** While mutual funds and ETFs expect you to buy-and-hold for years, waiting for market value growth, CEFs use a variety of strategies to multiply your income for higher distributions, usually monthly.

You can see that CEFs are the better income-producing retirement vehicle when you compare disbursement histories over time with those of other investment vehicles. Let's do that now.

CEFS: A MARKET MIRROR WITH HIGHER INCOME

One important thing to know about CEFs is that their market value performance tends to mirror stock market performance, interest-rate expectations, and trends in other key economic indicators.

They're not a countercyclical investment type. They don't go up when the stock market goes down, or when there's talk that interest rates will rise, or if the economy runs into trouble.

You can see how CEFs reflect what's going on in markets, interest rates, and the economy in the chart below.

What you're looking at is a comparison between one of the most highly regarded mutual funds, Vanguard Target Retirement Income Fund (VTINX), and a real estate focused CEF, Cohen & Steers Quality Income Realty (RQI).

I chose this high-leverage equity CEF fund to compare with the ultraconservative bond mutual fund to show how similar they are over the long haul. One could legitimately say that, over time, a leveraged equity CEF is equally as safe as a staid old-school bond mutual fund despite the additional volatility.

Note that these two funds start and end at a similar point, in relation to where they were a decade ago and to each other. A few fun facts about these two funds:

- This Vanguard fund is huge—it's one of the biggest funds you find in 401(k) plans.
- The Vanguard doesn't use leverage.
- The Vanguard current yield is 2.7 percent.
- The Cohen & Steers CEF's current yield is 8.3 percent.
- The CEF has much more volatility for profit-taking than the mutual fund.
- The CEF uses 30 percent leverage.
- The CEF is invested 75 percent in real estate companies.
- In 1Q 2023, the CEF's distributions were long term realized capital gains.

The bottom line: The CEF pays three *times as much income* as the Vanguard, with nearly the same long-term price history.

Let's look at another aspect of income-focused investing, I said. Which fund do you think had better profit-taking opportunities?

"It's the CEF, right?" Jean asked.

You got it, I said. That additional volatility means many more profit-taking opportunities!

Say you bought this CEF in 2013. Look at how its value went up over 40 percent from that cost basis right before the pandemic—and then sank to -20 percent when the pandemic hit. It also saw a huge spike at the start of 2022, right before interest rates began to rise. There were many smaller ups and downs over the years, too.

You could have easily traded this CEF five times in 2017-18 alone, pocketing more profits to reinvest. Remember, there aren't fees for trading anymore. You could consider selling if it were up just 2 percent and look for another opportunity to buy it lower in the future.

CEFS VS. THE MARKETS

The base-income and profit-taking advantages with CEFs aren't just evident when you compare them against mutual funds, either. Here's another example that compares CEF performance to one of the biggest stock market indices. They always tell you that you can't beat the S&P with active trading. Well, I'm about to prove that old saying wrong.

Look at this chart comparing a CEF with the S&P, in essence. It shows an ETF that buys the S&P—State Street Global Advisors' SPDR S&P 500 ETF (SPY)—and Kohlberg Kravis Roberts & Co.'s KKR Income Opportunities Fund CEF (KIO). Again, these two securities start at the same value and end at a similar place—in this case, roughly 150 percent above their starting point.

Why did I choose to compare a 94 percent bond fund with the S&P average? It's a kick to beat the S&P with a bunch of bonds!

Here are the fun facts about these two funds:

- The ETF doesn't use leverage.
- The S&P-based ETF's current yield is 1.6 percent.
- The CEF's current yield is 13.6 percent.
- The CEF is 41 percent leveraged.
- The CEF's shares have traded higher than SPY since early 2021.

Of course, the least volatile security is SPY, which simply tracks the S&P. As with our other example, the CEF is more volatile. Remember, CEFs are less liquid and trade fewer shares, and this is the main reason you'll see more spikes and drops.

"Look at that wild spike the CEF hit right before interest rates went up," John said. "Boy, you must have made some nice profits there!"

You bet I did. And I pointed out, there were great opportunities to lower your cost basis in this CEF from mid-2015 through 2017, too.

Almost nobody in our capitalist market environment gives a large profit percentage to their shareholders. Mutual funds and ETFs give potential market value gains now and then, so shareholders can build their egos and feel like they're getting rich. But few investors pull the trigger and turn paper profits into realized income.

Very few mutuals or ETFs produce significant money that you can spend, and too few investors even think to take profits on either. Income production is what CEFs are all about—and my credo of "Let no reasonable profit go unrealized" strengthens income production even further.

For the final proof of how CEFs beat mutual funds and ETFs, you have to look at what happens to your portfolio when you start making yearly 4 percent living-expense withdrawals. Let's look at that now.

FIFTEEN: What 4% Withdrawals Do to Different Portfolios

B Y N O W, I think you understand why I often say: "Market value fuels the ego; income fuels the yacht." Just to make sure you're still with me, what produces the income, market value or working capital?

"Working capital," the Cranes replied in unison.

That's right, I replied. I've got three charts I want to show you next that should drive home how income-focused investing provides better for you in retirement compared with traditional market value focused investing.

Investment professionals guesstimate that the normal portfolio drawdown in retirement will be around 4 percent of portfolio market value each year. The only required withdrawals are the RMDs (required minimum distributions) from tax-deferred retirement programs. That percentage rises each year, depending on life expectancy. Currently, the RMD at age 72 is just 3.5 percent.

Let's see where three different $500,000 portfolios got their needed 4 percent withdrawals from 2008 to 2021. Assume there was no additional income from capital gains during this time in any of the portfolios. Also, assume there were no deposits and that all forms of withdrawals are included in the 4 percent.

- PORTFOLIO ONE is a 50-50 mix of equity and income CEFs. The yield was around 10 percent as of March 2023. It holds ten CEFs that meet our QDI selection requirements, which were selected randomly by the chart's creator, investor Bryan Finnegan. (The specific CEFs in Portfolio One are available from the *Retirement Money Secrets Resource Guide* at theincomecoach.net.)
- PORTFOLIO TWO is the SPDR S&P 500 ETF Trust (SPY), yielding less than 2 percent. Looking at this ETF's performance is a quick way to see how the stock market performed during this time.
- PORTFOLIO THREE is the Vanguard Total Bond Market Index Fund (BND), yielding 2.57 percent. This is an easy way to review how the bond markets did in this time frame.

"Gotcha," John said.

COMPARING INCOME

This chart compares the base income generated by the three portfolios:

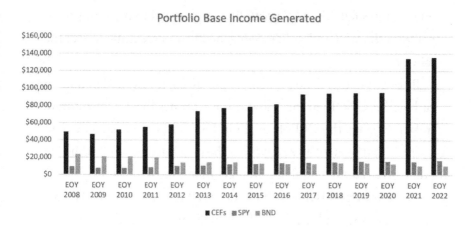

Portfolio Base Income Generated	CEFs	SPY	BND
EOY 2008	$49,319	$9,378	$23,241
EOY 2009	$46,510	$7,388	$20,936
EOY 2010	$51,730	$7,538	$20,804
EOY 2011	$54,961	$8,389	$19,668
EOY 2012	$57,999	$9,911	$13,893
EOY 2013	$73,287	$10,498	$14,326
EOY 2014	$76,778	$11,765	$14,557
EOY 2015	$78,531	$12,628	$13,003
EOY 2016	$81,751	$13,363	$12,498
EOY 2017	$93,057	$13,853	$12,579
EOY 2018	$94,031	$14,392	$13,318
EOY 2019	$94,379	$15,518	$13,452
EOY 2020	$94,832	$15,385	$12,198
EOY 2021	$134,116	$15,072	$10,264
EOY 2022	$135,677	$16,226	$10,464

The annual withdrawal rate at 4 percent of $500,000 is $20,000. The total varies each year with the market value of the portfolio, but the income doesn't.

Since income growth is their primary focus, it's no surprise that the CEF portfolio generates way more income than the S&P or bonds, every single year. Much more, in fact, than is needed for annual withdrawals.

In the bond results, you can see the impact of the interest-rate decline after the 2009-2010 financial crisis in the decreasing income. BND started above the 4 percent mark, but that changed quickly as interest rates fell. The SPY portfolio was doomed to dip into principal from the start and didn't even generate 4 percent income in the rally of 2021!

By contrast, there's no problem withdrawing the needed minimum cash with CEFs. Their income starts at 2.5 times the 4 percent draw. In fact, by 2015, the CEFs brought in four times more income than needed. And by 2021, it's seven times the necessary amount, while the others were still selling shares to meet minimum expenses.

My favorite part is that by the time we hit the pandemic and recovery years of 2021 and '22, the CEFs brought in even *more* income than before, thanks to reinvesting excess income. Meanwhile, income for SPY and BND languished.

Imagine having all that extra money to reinvest each year—or to cover you if you need to make more than 4 percent withdrawals, for any reason.

Remember, no realized capital gains are included in these charts. These are the results purely from base income and, in the case of the CEF portfolio, from reinvesting excess base income beyond 4 percent. If the CEF portfolio manager was profit-taking as usual, of course, that portfolio would show even more income.

DO 4% WITHDRAWALS CAUSE WORKING CAPITAL TO GROW OR SHRINK?

Retirees know they're likely to make 4 percent annual withdrawals. For traditional investors, that's funded mainly by what their investment professionals would call "returns"—meaning gains in market value.

But there's a problem: With most mutual funds or ETFs yielding less than 3 percent, they'll have to sell some securities to raise the rest of their withdrawals. Usually, they won't sell the "winners," which simply means those that have gone up in price. The resulting capital losses might give you a tax break, but they reduce your working capital. Not a good thing.

You might see 4 percent withdrawals from SPY that are nearly as large as those from the CEF portfolio, but there's a big difference. Most of SPY's cash comes from selling securities, while the CEFs' income covers expenses with a lot more left over. On the bond side, of course, withdrawals are going to be lower than either of the other two.

The chart below illustrates the amount of working capital drawdown (or excess withdrawals) seen by each of the three portfolios over the 15 years and the impact on our $500,000 of initial working capital. As the 4 percent withdrawals are made, you'll see that all but the CEF portfolio is losing working capital with every monthly payment.

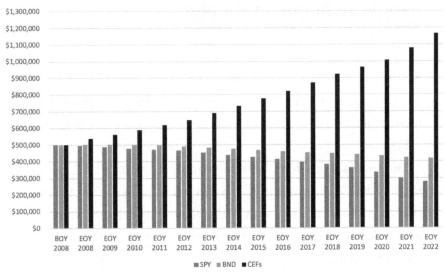

WC Growth vs Drawdown Analysis

	SPY	BND	CEFs
BOY 2008	$500,000	$500,000	$500,000
EOY 2008	$495,727	$501,509	$535,668
EOY 2009	$487,783	$501,182	$561,982
EOY 2010	$478,386	$500,308	$589,126
EOY 2011	$470,211	$497,516	$618,881
EOY 2012	$464,377	$489,167	$648,127
EOY 2013	$451,448	$482,590	$689,404
EOY 2014	$437,695	$475,912	$731,384
EOY 2015	$425,519	$468,416	$776,473
EOY 2016	$412,212	$460,738	$821,264
EOY 2017	$394,906	$453,257	$869,669
EOY 2018	$380,749	$447,340	$923,163
EOY 2019	$360,303	$440,695	$965,434
EOY 2020	$334,819	$432,111	$1,006,986
EOY 2021	$299,379	$422,796	$1,077,919
EOY 2022	$275,925	$416,949	$1,165,014

Let's unpack each portfolio's performance, one at a time.

The leftmost line shows SPY's working capital shrinking by more than $200,000 over 15 years. That's over 40 percent of the starting working capital—gone. Securities had to be sold to get money to help cover the 4 percent, since the S&P 500 only pays around 2 percent in dividends.

Talk about destructive return of capital! By 2022, this portfolio has less than $300,000 left to work with, to produce income for you in retirement. That's going to be tough unless you reposition them to produce income.

The middle line shows BND operating in the red as well, but by only about $80,000 (16 percent less). Why? It grew less in market value than the other portfolios, so minimum withdrawal needs were lower. Principal was invaded, but not nearly so much as with the S&P portfolio. But still, not heading in the right direction income-wise.

Finally, the line on the right shows the CEF portfolios' results. It never had a deficit and generated investable income every year, beyond the withdrawals. The total of nearly $600,000 in excess income by 2022 more than doubled starting working capital, with income growing every quarter.

To sum up: While S&P and bond investors face a future of shrinking income, CEF investors see ever more income, to either spend or reinvest as they please. Unless they make large withdrawals beyond their total income, their working capital and income keep on growing.

Let's compare these portfolios in one final way.

MARKET VALUE GROWTH OF THE 3 PORTFOLIOS

As income-focused investors, we don't rely on market value growth to pay our bills. But you'll remember that growth is the "cake" of the growth bucket of a CEF portfolio.

We're 50 percent in growth-purpose CEFs in this portfolio, so we should expect reasonable market value growth. We also want to compare that growth with the S&P and bond portfolios. Here's a chart with those results:

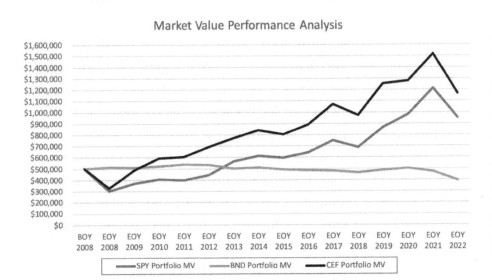

Market Value Performance Analysis

	SPY Portfolio MV	BND Portfolio MV	CEF Portfolio MV
BOY 2008	$500,000	$500,000	$500,000
EOY 2008	$303,326	$512,931	$327,621
EOY 2009	$367,964	$510,322	$484,696
EOY 2010	$406,434	$520,280	$590,061
EOY 2011	$397,543	$539,036	$604,939
EOY 2012	$442,670	$533,814	$690,062
EOY 2013	$562,255	$501,679	$768,246
EOY 2014	$612,431	$509,637	$839,470
EOY 2015	$595,295	$491,987	$802,610
EOY 2016	$640,068	$484,228	$887,035
EOY 2017	$747,807	$481,441	$1,071,642
EOY 2018	$685,181	$461,650	$972,876
EOY 2019	$863,144	$482,377	$1,250,588
EOY 2020	$980,862	$498,764	$1,278,708
EOY 2021	$1,212,291	$469,898	$1,516,404
EOY 2022	$952,315	$391,941	$1,165,961

First, you can see why professionals say bond-focused mutual funds don't cut it for retirement. BND's value went nowhere for most of our time span, then declined. It's definitely not leaving much for the heirs.

The market value growth of the S&P portfolio is clearly a force to be reckoned with. But remember, it has more financial and market risk than most retirees would want. We've all seen the devastation of a correction on market value-focused investors.

On the other hand, the CEF portfolio combines stocks and bonds in a well-diversified package with less risk, while delivering nearly four times the income.

The CEFs' net market value growth was ahead of both the other funds from sometime in 2011 through December 2021. *In that 14-year period, the CEF portfolio nearly tripled in market value.* It hit a higher market value high than the stock-only S&P 500 at the peak of the 2021 rally. You may want to stop and think about that.

You've heard that you've got to be in stocks to get market value growth—but in fact, the CEF portfolio reliably outstripped the S&P's growth. And that was with no profit-taking. Just think how even a small amount of targeted profit-taking would have accelerated CEF portfolio income and working capital growth over this time. The fact is capital gains in 2021 alone nearly equaled base income over my managed portfolios.

Which of these three portfolio types would you rather have? Which do you think best prepares you to cope with any unforeseen spending need, like a sudden itch for a globe-trotting vacation, a medical crisis, or your granddaughter's junior year abroad?

"No mystery there—it's the CEF portfolio," said Jean.

Exactly. I really want to demonstrate how this works for you, so let me show you the actual results for a couple of portfolios I managed for clients.

PART III

Examples of Building
Retirement Income

SIXTEEN: IFRI in Action: Results From 2 Professionally Managed CEF Portfolios

THINK THIS FIRST example is most relatable for anyone thinking about getting into CEFs for the first time. It's a portfolio I managed for someone who just got into CEFs in 2013. That's not so long ago.

A NEWBIE'S CEF EXPERIENCE

This client started with a portfolio of around $300,000. (If the chart looks familiar, it's because I used it in the Income discussion when we talked about Income Growth.)

As you can see, small can be mighty when you're invested in CEFs. Over the course of just nine years, the working capital in this portfolio more than doubled!

Note that these results were achieved without any new deposits. Figures are also net of management fees starting in 2017, when I was forced to begin charging for portfolio management due to compliance rules. About 40 percent of the portfolio is now in equity CEFs and 60 percent in income.

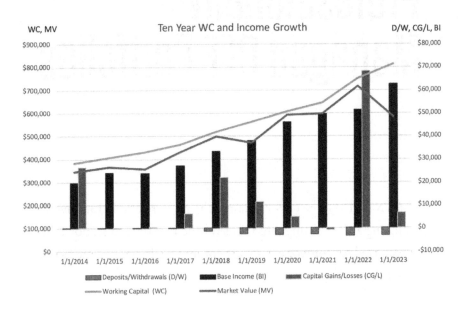

Note that the working capital line goes up steadily, while the market value line bounces around until 2022. During the correction, it moves significantly lower. Just look at the gap between working capital and market value!

At this point in your learning, you shouldn't be surprised that neither working capital nor income growth are affected by those market value changes.

Income growth perks up in 2019, as the final common-stock positions are sold. The common stocks were all what I called investment-grade value stocks—a group of about 250 NYSE companies that pay dividends, are profitable, and trade between $10 and $80.

It's easy to see the bounce in working capital from the 2021 rally. Better yet, income and capital continue to grow in the correction year 2022—supposedly the worst year for stocks since the Great Recession. Note the extra income growth in 2022, a direct result of the profit-taking orgy in 2021.

To sum up, this portfolio shows how even a newbie is protected from market gyrations with steady CEF income.

A RETIRED COUPLE'S MANAGED PORTFOLIO

Below are the stats for a retired couple in their late 70s. They have separate IRAs, which I've combined for this example. The average number of different securities over the years was about 80. Asset allocation was roughly 30 percent equity/70 percent income.

The CEFs were all chosen from within my IFRI selection universes. None of the securities accounted for as much as 4 percent of the total.

The chart below shows base income, capital gains, working capital, and market value over 5 years. Results are after RMD withdrawals, taxes, and management fees.

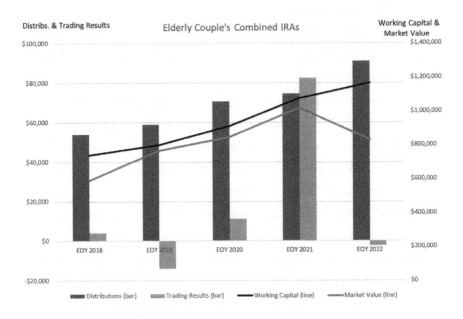

Yearly Results	Working Capital (line)	Market Value (line)	Distributions (bar)	Trading Results (bar)
EOY 2018	$739,996	$590,473	$53,938	$4,066
EOY 2019	$799,668	$767,383	$58,837	-$13,919
EOY 2020	$909,481	$846,246	$70,580	$11,190
EOY 2021	$1,074,386	$1,017,581	$74,629	$82,468
EOY 2022	$1,165,703	$831,216	$91,034	-$2,472

To unpack the stats across the five-year period:

- Working capital grew 58 percent.
- Market value increased 41 percent.
- Base income grew nearly 70 percent.
- Base income + capital gains = $430,000

- Total 2021 realized income was $157,000—a 14.6 percent yield on working capital.
- While market value declined during the 2022 correction, working capital grew by 8.5 percent and distributions rose by 22 percent.

You can see a listing of specific equity and income CEFs from this example in the Retirement Money Secrets Resource Guide.

This example shows how you don't invade principal with a CEF portfolio because of the tremendous income and working capital growth. But you *will* have to sell assets to pay bills with most 401(k), mutual fund, and ETF portfolios.

"Really, you can stop with the charts," Jean said, smiling. "We want to redo our portfolio and start investing in CEFs. We're just not sure how much help we're going to need doing it. How does it look if you set up a CEF portfolio and manage it yourself?"

Glad you asked, I replied. As it happens, I have a fitting example from my investor network.

SEVENTEEN: A Self-Managed IFRI Portfolio in Action

THE EXAMPLE BELOW shows you can do well with CEFs even if you don't do all the frequent profit-taking that's a key part of my own CEF portfolio management.

This investor had a large portfolio and decided she didn't want to be bothered checking the markets regularly for profit-taking opportunities. She just left many of her CEFs alone to generate income and grow in market value. She stuck her head in monthly to reinvest base income but felt no need to accelerate income growth with constant profit-taking. Her results prove that even partial involvement in CEFs can yield excellent results if the basic QDI principles are well-executed.

A BIGGER INVESTOR'S DIY PORTFOLIO

Her CEF journey began in 2008. This is a CEF-transition portfolio—she's still not 100 percent into CEFs, as she waits for older ETFs and individual stocks to regain prior highs. She enjoys owning multiple types of securities and can afford to live with less income than she knows is possible.

It's interesting to see how well she did, even though she could have earned more if she'd taken profits when market value exceeded working capital. In this period, neither income nor working capital were maximized, but the portfolio still did very well. That's because she used basic QDI principles in selecting all securities, even the non-CEFs.

Look at the growth of both withdrawals and distribution income through two major and one mini- correction!

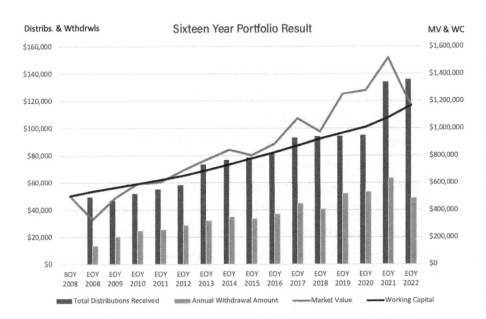

In 2018, you see income growth slowing while market value peaks higher than working capital. Most of those profits were lost in 2022 with the market correction. This is why I love regular profit-taking—but not everyone suffers emotionally like I do when a profit goes unrealized.

She tells me, "Steve, I don't do this every day like you." And you don't have to if you have a large enough portfolio. The earlier you start, the sooner you'll have enough income where you don't have to look for profit-taking opportunities every day.

She continues to selectively reinvest about 50 percent of the income. She can afford to. That's the secret of this portfolio's success. As long as you don't spend all your income and keep reinvesting, you're in good shape.

This portfolio shows that DIY is exactly that. You decide how much of the IFRI program you want to do—you can implement the whole program, or just enough to accomplish your own goals. Clearly, this investor isn't hard-up for spending cash and understands the process.

EIGHTEEN: Making the Switch to CEFs

"**W**E'RE SOLD," JOHN said. "But how do you convert your IRA from a traditional portfolio into an income focused CEF investment portfolio?"

Investors are in three typical scenarios when they get started with CEFs:

1. You've got a lump of cash and want to use it to start a CEF portfolio.
2. You have an existing portfolio and want to gradually switch part of it into CEFs.
3. You have an existing portfolio and want to switch it all into CEFs.

No matter which of these scenarios applies, there are a few basic steps you need to take, I explained. If you want to invest in CEFs, your first step is always to create your selection universes. Follow our QDI rules and develop diversified income and equity CEF collections that meet all the criteria we've discussed.

Once you have those, you determine your asset allocation. Are you young and risk-taking enough to be 70 percent in growth-purpose securities? Or are you at or near retirement and seeking mostly income focused CEFs? Or somewhere in between?

If there are multiple parts to your portfolio—maybe you've got an IRA, a Roth IRA, a personal trading account, and a 401(k)—remember to consider how all the parts are invested in order to create the diversified asset mix you want.

Finally, are we talking about $100,000 or a million? Every portfolio is different. From here the strategies diverge, so let me walk you through them one at a time.

NINETEEN: Switching a Cash Account into CEFs

S WITCHING FROM CASH into income focused CEF investing is the easiest of the three transition scenarios.

Say you just received an inheritance. If you've made your asset allocation decisions and created CEF universes for both growth and income, you're ready to select specific CEFs.

The key is to go slowly. You're not going to buy $100,000 worth of equities on the first day, I hope! Or put $10,000 into a single CEF. You buy a little of each, each day. We've talked about the market cycle and how its position will help with your decision-making. To start, buy maybe one-third of the amount you may eventually want in a single holding.

This is a good time to look at the risk pyramid you learned about in our diversification discussion. If you want to limit risk, you should start investing in the safest types of CEFs—the ones at the bottom of the pyramid.

I'm talking about CEFs that hold federal securities, corporate bonds, and preferred stocks for smaller portfolios. Moving into sector funds, global equity or bond funds, and IT equities may be best for larger commitments. Look inside the CEF and make sure you like how it's invested. Then, make several selections, but you don't have to own everything in the universe.

INVESTING HIGH, INVESTING LOW

Remember to stay well below 5 percent of working capital on any single security. Usually, you should leave lots of room to add to positions at lower prices, especially if we're at or near what appears to be a market high.

If you want to invest your money in CEFs quickly and the market's high, I'd advise patience. You don't want to rush in, then see values go down, leaving few profit-taking opportunities. It also hurts to see that if you'd been patient, you could have gotten into your securities at a lower cost and a higher yield.

On the other hand, if you're at or near a market bottom, you might go a bit faster. I'd go as high as 2 percent on the initial purchase in a smallish portfolio, but as little as 1 percent in a jumbo portfolio. For instance, it's more likely the market will go up than down if we're well into a correction. The opposite is true when we've been in a long-term rally.

Bit by bit, fill your buckets. Once you buy, watch to see if your holdings go up in price. If they go up a reasonable amount based on portfolio size and market conditions, you know what to do, right?

"Sell," Jean said.

Exactly. Repeat until all your money is invested, except for a contingency reserve for known monthly withdrawals and emergencies. Put your investment money to work, and keep your contingency reserves separate. It doesn't matter how much cash you still have to invest—leave no reasonable profit unrealized.

TWENTY: Partial Transition From an Existing Portfolio

"I WISH WE WERE sitting on a pile of cash," John said. "But our retirement money is all invested the traditional way, mostly in mutual funds and ETFs. Where would I even begin to switch over?"

Great question, I said. If you just want to test the water and put some of your working capital into CEFs, you'll go little by little. Find the most speculative positions in your existing portfolio and switch them into CEFs first. It's time to look through your current portfolio to see if you have any dangerous positions.

"What does that mean?" Jean asked.

Do you own any individual stocks with prices that have gone sky-high? Any securities that have grown to over 5 percent of working capital, perhaps through DRIP programs?

It's time to liquidate at least part of these, take some profits, and get better diversified. Put the net proceeds into CEFs from your selection universes.

If you have a large stake in some old, inherited security in a taxable account that would be 90 percent capital gain if you sell it now, set up a 5-year plan to gradually divest. Spread your tax bite over a few years—except when the market is really low. Then, move quickly to jump on the lower prices.

Also look at any outliers. Do you have 100 shares of some fly-by-night thing you got a hot tip on in a bar once in your youth, and it's never gone anywhere? Take your losses and put the money into CEFs.

Remember, if you have non-taxable accounts in your portfolio, you can take some profits and start to reinvest in higher-yielding CEFs without creating a tax bill. Your current yield is probably around 2 percent, and you want 6 percent or more. Monitor what happens as you add income CEFs, and you'll see progress toward your goal.

Make sure the traditional side of your portfolio contains only the best-quality securities, and add CEFs to that.

HOW MUCH IS ENOUGH?

"How much of your portfolio would you need to switch into CEFs for this hybrid investing scheme to make sense?" John asked.

If you put $100,000 into CEFs, you're giving it a chance, I replied. That'll be enough positions that you can start to see the difference it's making. If you have a larger portfolio, you could get to 25 percent or so in CEFs. Then, study the results for a while before deciding whether to go further.

You'll also want to tell your broker—or put a reminder on your calendar if you do your own trades—to check regularly for when your securities get into a profit position. Then, you can decide what action is necessary.

Profit-taking gives you fresh cash you can use to add to CEFs where prices have declined or to put into additional CEFs from your selection universes. Over time, that'll increase the percent of your portfolio that's invested in CEFs.

"Profit-taking intrigues me," John said. "I know I want to start taking some profits and see how that grows my portfolio. I absolutely can see the benefits.

"How does this work if you know that you want to switch your whole portfolio to CEFs? I think that's what we want to do."

TWENTY-ONE: Going All-In on CEFs

E XCITING—I LOVE WORKING with investors who're all-in on converting to CEFs. This process has three steps and takes about a month to complete. Let me go over those steps first. Then I have an example to show you. I recently switched a traditional portfolio into CEFs in a month flat, so I've got a quick case study.

THREE STEPS TO AN ALL-CEF PORTFOLIO

Here is my process for converting a traditional portfolio to an income focused CEF portfolio.

Step One: Do your research, create universes for growth and income CEFs using our QDI principles, and decide on your asset allocation plan. Once that's in place, you're ready to start switching your working capital to CEF investing.

Step Two for personal portfolios: If your taxable investment account has substantial unrealized capital gains, establish a 5-year or less program to realize the gains. Invest the net after-tax proceeds in CEFs. The time frame depends on several factors, including your tax bracket, needed income, years to retirement, and availability of offsetting losses. You don't want to sell out everything at once without offsetting losses, because that could trigger a high capital-gains tax bill.

Step Two for qualified plans: If your funds are in a tax-sheltered retirement plan, such as a rollover IRA or a tax-free Roth IRA, you can move faster. The first step is to sell any high-risk positions, take any significant unrealized profits, and start buying CEFs. One caveat here: Don't sell everything all at once, generating more cash than can be quickly reinvested. We don't want money sitting around uninvested for a long time. but a week or so is fine. Eventually, all sales proceeds are invested in your diversified CEF portfolio.

You'll want to sell more quickly in an "up" market to lock in gains but buy smaller amounts when reinvesting. In a "down" market, you may sell the lowest-yielding positions first, but it's inevitable that you'll experience some losses on your existing positions.

Study the fundamentals and hold on to high-quality equities a bit longer but be prepared to sell if your income goals are not yet met. In a correction, you may wind up selling them all at losses so you can take advantage of the opportunity to buy CEFs at lower costs and higher yields.

Step Three: Now, you're doing two things at once. You're operating an active IFRI portfolio—including taking profits and reinvesting—and slowly replacing all the remaining non-CEF securities.

- Continue to prioritize profit-taking in liquidating your positions, even if it creates capital gains. Remember, an after-tax 65 percent profit is better than no profit.
- Next, get rid of the lowest-quality, highest-risk, and lowest income-producing securities. Possibly, some losses here will help offset gains on the profit-taking side.
- Continue taking profits and cutting losers until all the non-CEF securities are gone.

"Sounds simple enough," said Jean. "Interested to see your example of how this works in an actual portfolio."

EXAMPLE: CONVERTING A $1M MIXED PORTFOLIO INTO CEFS

I converted a $1 million IRA portfolio into CEFs in 2018. The starting asset allocation was 60 percent equity vs. 40 percent income. The portfolio contained a few individual equities, some ETFs, and mutual funds. We anticipated an additional $180,000 deposit would arrive shortly, bringing the working capital to nearly $1 million.

The total income production was less than $17,000, or 2.2 percent. Don't get me started on how low that yield is! To see the actual positions in this portfolio, go to the Retirement Money Secrets Resource Guide.

My initial analysis showed five positions were larger than $50,000, which exceeded 5 percent of total working capital. There was $35,000 in unrealized gains, but few funds that concerned me—just two hedge funds, because they're inherently more risky than other forms of investment.

My transition priorities were to:

- Eliminate the two higher-risk funds.
- Take profits starting with the largest positions.
- Reverse the asset allocation to 70 percent income purpose vs. 30 percent growth, which is more appropriate for a retiree.
- Reduce the exposure in the five oversized positions.

The proceeds were gradually reinvested to hit our 30 percent equity, 70 percent income asset allocation target mix.

THE TRANSITION

Within three weeks, most of the original positions were sold and replaced with CEFs that met my QDI criteria. Within five months, the CEFs generated nearly $22,000 in distribution income—25 percent more than the old portfolio would have generated *in an entire year*.

Additionally, $60,000 in capital gains were realized. This came mostly from gradually selling existing positions, plus three rapid turnovers of freshly purchased CEFs. Their prices rose soon after I bought them, so they were sold at a profit, adding to working capital.

4 YEARS LATER

At year-end 2022, working capital was nearly $1,445,000 after all RMD distributions and fees—a $400,000 gain over four years. The 2022 correction-year distribution total was particularly satisfying: $93,169 up from $88,769 in the 2021 rally year.

SUMMARY: In 4.5 years, the portfolio's working capital grew by more than 40 percent and was generating nearly 9 percent in annual distributions. Base income was just under $125,000 a year. There was nearly $96,000 in realized capital gains in 2021 alone.

"Wow. Nearly half a mil more working capital in the portfolio in under five years and seven times the base income! That's impressive," John said.

"I feel like I've learned so much from you, and I'm really interested in CEF investing. Is it crazy that I still feel like I have a lot of questions? And I know our time is up."

Not at all, I said. In fact, I'm having a Zoom Q&A with The Income Coach Facebook group next week. I'll send you the link, and you can participate.

"That'd be great," John said. "See you online!"

PART IV

Investing for More
Retirement Money–Q&A

TWENTY-TWO: But I've Still Got Questions

B ACK IN SOUTH Carolina, I adjusted my headset and got ready for my monthly Q&A Zoom call with my Facebook group. When I went live, I was happy to see the Cranes were indeed logged in to participate.

The questions came fast and furious in the chat. Longtime member Will Allender read the questions off to me:

Q: What's a reasonable minimum starting amount of capital needed to make the IFRI (Income Focused Retirement Income) strategy work for a retiree or a soon-to-be?

I don't have a single answer, as there are many variables. For instance, what other income sources do you have—a pension, rents, Social Security?

In general, this process works best for two types of investors:

- People in their early investing years who want to build an income bucket along with their stock market exposure.
- People at or approaching retirement age who have accumulated significant funds and want to make them produce so much income that they never have to dip into principal.

If you insist on a dollar figure, I'd say you need at least $100,000 for this strategy to succeed. You need to establish quite a few different positions, to get enough diversity. Then you can compare performance and adjust productively as you go.

Q: Is dipping into principal always bad? What if I have a very large portfolio?

It can work if someone with a large portfolio nibbles away at principal without killing a problematic amount of income. If they're quite elderly and have reached the point where they're not traveling or spending much, maybe it's a tipping point where minor capital erosion isn't a big deal. That's especially true if you're not worried about providing for heirs.

Everyone who's still saving for retirement or trying to live an active lifestyle in retirement where you spend big for travel or hobbies, you want to avoid invading principal. Over time, it'll result in less working capital. That's not good if you still need substantial income.

Q: How do I physically buy or sell securities in a smart way? I've never done this.

Great question—especially because CEFs are a smaller, less liquid market than other types of securities. That means it's important to do "day limit" orders.

A day-limit order is a buy or sell order that expires at the end of the day. You specify how many shares you want and the maximum price you're willing to pay, or the number of shares you wish to sell and the minimum you'll accept from the buyer. Using a day limit, you'll often buy a security for less than expected or sell for more than expected. It's the only order type I ever place.

While we're talking about orders, you may also use open-limit orders at target prices. They stay open until either executed or canceled. I never do these for many reasons.

Finally, there's one type of order you should never do with CEFs, because of their relatively small numbers of outstanding shares. That's a "market" order. "At the market" means you're willing to buy or sell at whatever the next price is that someone asks or offers.

This price could be vastly different from what you have in mind. It can change a good buy to a mistake or a profit to a loss. Brokers tend to place all their orders "at the market," so make it a point to give your broker specific instructions as to order type.

Q: How do you take profits and keep your velocity of money moving if everything is going down in value?

There are times when profits are slim to none. It's a fact of investing life.

If it's a time like that, focus on base income. Plan on spending no more than 60 percent of it, and you can continue to have income growth. There won't always be capital gains.

The 2021 capital gains were, in some cases, more than base income. By contrast, in 2023, I'm forecasting that my former customers' accounts won't hit $1 million in total capital gains, compared with $7 million in 2021.

You need reserves to survive a prolonged correction. If you're going to the Bahamas in April, make sure you're accumulating the capital you need months in advance.

Q: How are the fees on CEFs overcome by the higher returns?

It's a misconception that shareholders pay any of the expenses listed for CEFs. They don't.

What do you mean by "returns"? That's Wall Street-ese for "market value going up," which isn't even our goal.

Not one of my former clients was ever charged a fee by any of their CEFs. That's what the company—the trust—pays the manager. A fund's income production beyond their costs is what we receive in distributions. Our "returns" are stable, continual, and of the realized variety.

Q. How about the fees charged by advisors in managed accounts and model portfolios?

There's a big difference between the two. A professional advisor manages each portfolio separately. That's what I did for nearly 45 years. Total advisory fees are usually divided between the firm executing the trades and the independent advisor that directly serves the client.

In my case, fees ranged between 1.3 percent to 2 percent, depending upon portfolio size. Larger accounts paid less, and my portion of the fee was roughly 60 percent. In my firm, our goal was to make more in capital gains for the client than he or she paid in fees.

I recently read that model-portfolio managers are receiving as much as 2 percent in fees. I think that's ridiculous, quite frankly. Models are about the same as mutual funds. One size fits all, and there's no individual portfolio attention. Fees should be much lower.

I had a situation recently where an investor in a model portfolio told me he was only paying .5 percent—and his account was individually managed. Looking deeper, we discovered he was paying 1.5 percent for a model portfolio managed identically for thousands of people.

That said, I've developed a CEF model that's non-DRIP and aggressively managed using my principles. I'm looking for a firm that wants to buy it.

Q: Why not buy-and-hold CEFs, instead of flipping them after only a roughly 5 percent profit?

Think of it this way: If you have about 100 CEFs in each of your universes and they're paying an average of 9 percent, that's just .75 percent per month.

Even a 1 percent profit is more than your monthly distribution from that security. Taking a profit of more than .75 increases your total income for the year—and increases working capital.

Also, quicker profits increase the velocity of money without damaging overall yield, since there are plenty of new positions to choose from. I've never once had to accept a yield below 6 percent in purchasing income CEFs, whether the market was booming or in a correction. There are always opportunities. As I write this in May '23, with the markets still in a correction, I have over 200 CEFs I could buy right now at 9 percent or more.

So never let a profit of more than 5 percent go unrealized and take smaller profits when yield opportunities are abundant.

Q: If one of my CEFs is producing an outrageous yield of 9 percent and I can buy more at a lower-cost basis, why not add to it hot and heavy—even if it becomes more than 5 percent of my portfolio?

First, there's nothing outrageous about a 9 percent yield when you invest in CEFs!

Letting any one security grow to more than 5 percent of your holdings is just bad portfolio management. You're not properly diversified.

Don't allow greed to manage your portfolio. It may seem like a good idea at the time to overweight a strong performer but remember that the worm always turns. You'll regret it in the end.

Q: Should I include tax-free income CEFs in a Roth IRA?

There's no reason to unless we're talking about a portfolio over $5 million where you need additional diversification. Talk to your accountant about the tax consequences of putting particular types of CEFs into different types of retirement accounts. In general, there's no benefit to putting lower-yielding tax-free bonds into an already tax-free shell. Roth IRAs are the perfect vehicle for all the IFRI strategies, both income generation and profit-taking. It's easy to design one today with a 9 percent tax-free yield!

Q: What makes some CEFs trade at discounts, while others trade at premiums?

Remember, CEFs are not designed to trade at their NAV. Investor demand dictates their prices. At any given time, some are just more popular than others, based on investor sentiment about various investment types. It's how all individual securities are priced—there's no direct relationship between CEF price and the NAV. This is a more realistic relationship than exists in either ETFs or mutual funds.

The classic example would be a CEF full of Treasury bills yielding 2 percent with current interest rates over 5 percent. All are down in price because of higher rates. All will pay face value when they mature. Clearly current price and the impact on the NAV are of no consequence, but the yield on the CEF is now much higher.

Q: What's the difference between yield and return?

Yield is the amount of income received from a CEF divided by your cost. Return is the amount of growth in a security's market value. It serves no purpose at all until the "return" is realized.

Q: What can I really expect in terms of "realized returns"?

Here in spring 2023, the average yield on the 200+ CEFs in my income and growth selection universes is over 10 percent with nothing lower than 6 percent when anticipated full-year distributions are considered. Depending on your risk tolerance, you could construct a diversified CEF portfolio generating from 8 percent to 10 percent. Total realized return depends on the market cycle and how cutthroat you are when it comes to taking profits when they're available.

Q: Which CEF fund managers are the best and using what criteria?

To answer this, I'd have to know what form of measurement you prefer. There are 50 or more *providers* of CEFs. The dozen managers with the most funds (and experience) are at these companies:

- Aberdeen
- BlackRock
- Calamos
- Duff & Phelps
- Eaton Vance
- First Trust
- Gabelli
- Invesco
- John Hancock
- Nuveen
- PIMCO
- Western Asset

You can always assess a management's track record by looking at CEF performance over time. Regardless of who the manager is, I almost never buy a fund less than five years old, and never one with less than 50 securities inside.

You should also hold funds from multiple providers for better diversification. You should spread your investments between the 40 major CEF providers. It's just safer.

If you want to get more granular, look inside the fund. You can see the strategies they use, what they invest in, and their results. I think managers at bigger companies who oversee bigger funds have more to lose, so I trust them more.

Q: Why would I sell a CEF and take profits to buy another one that might not do as well?

We have no clue what the future will bring or for how long one CEF will "do better" than another. If you're walking down the sidewalk and you see a $100 bill, do you pick it up or walk on by? You'd never think you could come back tomorrow and still get that money.

In the same way, there's no reason to assume the profit you could take now will still be there tomorrow.

If you've followed the IFRI selection guidelines you've learned, it's reasonable to assume that new things you buy will also become profitable. If not, they're still doing their main job of income production.

Q: If I'm selling, should the replacement CEF be in the same asset class or a different one?

The smaller the portfolio, the more carefully selected your next position should be to maintain diversification. If you have a broadly diversified selection universe and at least 40 to 50 CEFs in your portfolio, it's not as much of a worry.

In any case, you could always choose some new CEF type or sector for reinvestment. It'll depend on your asset allocation—your decision is guided by whether you need to further diversify or rebalance.

Q: What is a Z-score? How do I compute it, and can it help me evaluate CEFs?

Z-scores are a kind of future prediction technology that compares a CEF's present premium or discount with its average premium/discount during a particular period.

I've never felt the need to know a Z-score, and nothing can really predict the future anyway. You can just look at the performance chart. You can look up Z-scores online, but I think they are of limited use.

Remember, CEF prices are determined by supply and demand. And different investors/speculators look for different things from their CEFs. We're looking for income and profit potential.

If I'm buying a long-experienced CEF that pays 8 percent a year, I couldn't care less if its current price is above or below its normal relationship to NAV—which, by the way, has no relationship to market price anyway.

For instance, here's a chart for the John Hancock Tax-Advantaged Dividend Income Fund CEF (HTD):

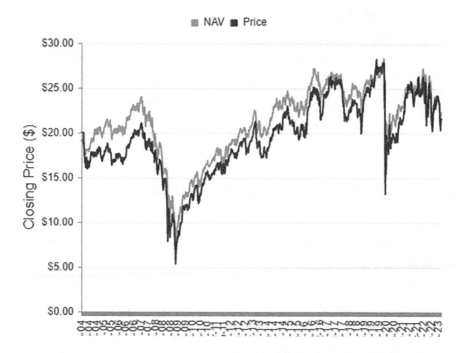

It's clear there's a close relationship between this CEF's price and the NAV—and it's been that way for 20 years.

What I want to see is price volatility that offers trading opportunities. You can clearly see this CEF has price volatility. In over 40+ years, I've never once needed to know anything about Z- scores.

Q: How are CEFs able to have such high yields? Are these sustainable, or are they a dividend-yield trap?

A dividend-yield trap occurs when a very high-dividend yield attracts investors to a potentially troubled company. It's a term that applies to individual common stocks, not to CEFs. A CEF can't be a yield trap because it contains hundreds of different securities of varying types, yields, maturities, and sectors.

Not all companies that pay a high-dividend yield are in trouble, but investors should question why a company is paying so much more than its peers. Some CEFs have paid the same yield for 60 years. A long track record paying the same or similar yield makes it clear CEF yields are sustainable and not a trap.

Q: Are CEFs only advisable in IRAs and Roth IRAs?

Absolutely not. They're essential in all areas of your investment port-folio. Your separate accounts complement each other and allow for better overall diversification. I use a taxable personal account to collect and reinvest monthly RMD payments from my two IRAs.

Other investors I know accumulate enough extra cash from CEF distributions in their personal accounts to fund the tax bite from Roth conversions. Again, consult with an accountant about this idea. But think about it: You could be earning 8 percent to 10 percent in tax-free income from your Roth IRA. If I had known about CEFs sooner, I would have converted my IRAs to Roths, which would now be three times the size and totally tax free.

Q: What's the best way to decide when to trade between similar pairs of CEFs?

Unless you have a small portfolio, there's no real need to avoid owning similar CEFs. I'd avoid buying them at the same time for diversification reasons. But in larger portfolios, why not have two similar CEFs?

It's unlikely that any pair is identical—and as an investor, you won't deal with them identically, either. You'll buy or sell based on their yield and market value changes.

Q: How do you determine if you've met diversification requirements?

The first step is to determine the total working capital in your portfolio. Then decide what percentage you're comfortable with.

Less than 3 percent per position is a good starting point. Then check the cost basis of your largest positions against your working capital figure to make sure no one position is too large.

Q: How can I avoid funds that will keep decreasing distributions and NAV for decades?

When you create your selection universe, you study a CEF's distribution history. It's clear when a downward trend is in process, so you can easily avoid any CEF that displays this pattern. If you own it, you can see this trend quickly and get rid of that sucker!

There is no direct relationship between distribution history and NAV. NAV is simply the market value of the securities within the fund.

If you develop doubts about a CEF, remove it from your selection universe. If you own it and it becomes unproductive, sell it. Remember, we don't keep CEFs for decades! We look for profit-taking opportunities and take them. I've rarely been disappointed enough to take a loss.

Q: Are there any financial advisors who specialize in managing CEF portfolios?

I only know of one company that manages portfolios in the way I have, constructed almost exclusively with CEFs. You can contact me through The Income Coach website if you're interested in more information about them.

I'm sure there are brokers or advisors who'd be willing to use CEFs in your managed portfolios with them, but it's likely you'd have to educate them to arouse any enthusiasm. There are firms that use CEF model portfolios exclusively, but I'm fairly certain none of them use the methods described here.

Q: If I'm going to do profit-taking, won't the trading fees eat into my profits?

Good news: Trading fees aren't a major issue these days—not even on broker-assisted trades.

Most brokerage firms no longer charge commissions, or many nuisance fees, until you ask for specific security advice or broker-assisted trades. If they consult with you, you pay for it.

But remember, your typical broker doesn't know much about CEF investing. Don't ask them for help in selection or execution—you'd have to help *them*.

It's truly a great time to be a CEF investor now that fees have been hammered down to near zero. Back in the '80s, I'd pay a 2 percent commission on all buy and sell equity transactions and a 3 percent markup on bonds. Now, investors can be active traders with little cost.

If you're buying or selling individual bonds, however, make sure you check for markups. They still exist, and you can avoid them totally with CEFs.

Q. What do you mean by almost exclusively CEFs?

In some of my larger portfolios, and my own, I use three ETFs that invest mostly in CEFs and have acceptable yields and trading opportunities. I also have four ETFs with exceptionally high yields and broad diversification. Again, I just have ETFs in larger portfolios that need additional diversification.

Q: How do I know if I'm doing this whole process right?

There are three key indicators that your CEF investing is going well:

1. **ANALYZE YOUR QUARTERLY BASE INCOME TOTALS.** They should be rising each quarter—and definitely each year.
2. **LOOK AT YOUR QUARTERLY WORKING CAPITAL TOTALS.** They should also rise each quarter—and absolutely must each year.
3. **COMPARE MARKET VALUE WITH WORKING CAPITAL, AT LEAST MONTHLY.** In most situations and for most investors, working capital should always be greater than market value.

If any of these checks reveal a problem—sinking base income or working capital, or market value higher than working capital—that's a big red flag that something's gone wrong in executing the six IFRI principles. It's time to call an expert consultant for a check-up.

TWENTY-THREE: Do It Yourself or Hire a Pro: A Quiz

A T THE END of the Q&A, I asked the Cranes to stay on the call. Now that you understand all the fundamentals of CEF investing, I said, there's only one decision left to make. Is CEF investing for you?

"We definitely think it is," John said. Jean nodded.

That's exciting! I replied. If that's the case, the next step is to decide how you want to do it.

There are three options:

1. **DIY:** Take what you've learned, build your own CEF universes with our QDI principles, and invest in the positions you like. Take profits, reinvest, and assess your own performance. Follow the system on your own. Doing it yourself can certainly increase your income and working capital growth, and you avoid paying management fees.

2. **DIY WITH HELP:** You do the daily portfolio management, but periodically consult with someone more experienced. Get a pro to advise you if you want help in building investment universes, profit-taking and reinvestment decisions, or progress assessments. Coaching is far less costly than hiring a firm to manage your portfolio full time.

3. **HIRE A PRO:** Enjoy your life and let a professional CEF investor manage your portfolio. If you don't want to have to think about your portfolio every day, the fees may be worth it, especially if you can find someone who'll focus on growing working capital and income, and aggressively look for enough profits to more than cover the fees.

How do you know which option is right for you? Here are some questions to help guide your decision.

HOW MUCH TIME CAN I DEVOTE TO HANDS-ON INVESTING?

Saving on fees sounds great, I know. But managing your own portfolio is a substantial time commitment and a big responsibility. And you may have to pay for sophisticated portfolio-management tools.

By going the DIY route, you take on all the tasks of the professional managers that take care of selection, diversification, and profit-taking in exchange for their 1.5 percent to 2 percent of your market value each year. Those managers put in full days studying markets and executing profit-taking strategies. Do you want to do that? Keep in mind that it'll probably take you *longer* than it takes them, since it's not your career.

Here's my own experience: Now that I've transitioned from managing 300+ portfolios as a full-time manager to a four-portfolio investor (with a side gig coaching new and less-experienced investors), I don't spend nearly as much time placing buy and sell orders. As a professional manager, I placed hundreds of orders on a busy day.

For my own portfolio, I still manage some significant amounts, maintain my selection universes, and monitor distribution activity. I still track my income, working capital, and market value numbers. I reinvest monthly distributions ASAP. In my case, that takes a few hours a day, most days.

If you have a smaller portfolio, there's less time required once you're up to speed. Everything doesn't have to be done daily, except perhaps checking for profits.

AM I UP FOR FREQUENTLY CHECKING ON MARKET ACTIVITY?

There are so many online brokerage platforms and apps available with in-depth portfolio detail that it's easy to review your portfolio from anywhere in the world. But for some people, looking daily at the stock market's gyrations produces severe indigestion. It's better for their mental health to delegate market monitoring to a pro.

On the other hand, if you start your day checking the indices and never miss *Squawk Box*, *Mad Money*, or whatever your favorite stock-analysis show is, the DIY option might work for you. You're hooked on following the markets anyway, so it's not much of an additional time commitment. Note, though, that those stock pundits almost never mention CEFs—that research is still on you. Their only real use is to confirm your judgment about where we are in the market cycle.

As a DIY-er, if you aren't in touch with your portfolio several times a day, you will absolutely miss out on profit-taking opportunities. How frequently you need to check depends upon market-cycle dynamics. Otherwise, the lost capital gains may become a considerable number over time—profits that are gone, possibly forever.

Maybe you're like the large-portfolio client I featured in the "IFRI in Action" chapter, and you don't need to be 100 percent focused on profit-taking. You have enough invested or aren't yet taking withdrawals. Then, you just let base income grow and don't have to watch the markets as often for profit-taking opportunities.

The more base income you need to withdraw for spending money, the more time you need to spend watching the markets. If you have high income needs and a small portfolio, you'd need to conduct daily market monitoring to avoid missing opportunities for capital gains.

DOES TRADING STRESS ME OUT?

Some people can make tough decisions in complex situations and never look back. For others, it's very stressful. Trading stocks is one of these situations.

How would you handle that stress, trading on your own—are you decisive enough to not second-guess yourself? Or would you be haunted by shoulda-coulda-woulda regrets? Might analysis paralysis derail your investment efforts?

Investing is a world of uncertainty. The only certainty is uncertainty itself. Not even the highest-paid professionals, TV show entertainers, or reporters have any clue what will happen tomorrow, or even a few minutes later today.

To buy your own securities, to trade at all, you have to operate in this environment and set reasonable performance standards and expectations for yourself. Think about whether you could do that.

WHAT'S MY RISK APPETITE FOR EXECUTING PROFIT-TAKING TRADES?

In the world of CEF investing, there's more risk in *not* taking profits than in taking them.

Not selling is the real gamble. You may miss an opportunity.

Remember, there's no such thing as a bad profit—or a good loss. If you sell, you pocket the money and have a chance to spread it around to new or old positions.

If you tend to "chicken out," this may not be for you. Unlike common stocks, with CEFs you're buying and selling portfolios of securities. The financial risk is minimized in several ways, because equally reliable and productive reinvestment opportunities are plentiful.

Knowing all that, if you're still paralyzed into inaction when faced with trading opportunities, DIY investing may not be for you.

DO I TRUST SOMEONE ELSE TO RUN MY PORTFOLIO?

Entrusting your portfolio to a manager takes faith and trust that this person will keep your best interests in mind. Most large firms pressure their sales employees to sell investment securities for specific monetary rewards. You should question if they're operating in your interests, their own, or the company's.

You eliminate that problem if you tell them what to invest in.

My challenge was always to make more in capital gains for each of my clients than they paid me in annual fees. In 2021, the capital gains in my clients' portfolios would have paid every client's total fees for the next 4+ years!

In my opinion, the smaller the firm, the more likely you'll be able to find someone you can trust to put you first. It's also more likely that a small-firm advisor will understand your attraction to income-focused CEFs.

Here's why 60-year-old Robin Fleetwood made his DIY decision. Robin was previously retired but is now running a hobby business and living off the distributions from his CEFs.

> "I opened a small brokerage account a few years ago, strictly to invest in CEFs for more diversification. I'd been managing about 60 percent of my portfolio, while my IRA remained with an

independent broker. When he died suddenly of COVID, rolling over the IRA and managing the transition to CEFs myself was a no-brainer. Nobody cares more about your money than you do."

As Robin found, if you already have some experience managing other parts of your portfolio, you may feel confident enough to take full charge of your CEF investing.

HOW DO I FEEL ABOUT THE FEES PROS CHARGE FOR PORTFOLIO MANAGEMENT?

When you hire an investment pro, you expect them to spend whatever time it takes to qualify all the investments, maintain diversification, generate income, and take profits. You pay a hefty sum for this service. Hands-on management can cost more than 2 percent per year, depending upon portfolio size. Model portfolios can be just as expensive, which, as I explained earlier, is a rip-off on many levels.

Fees can feel worrisome when your "manager" simply puts you into mutual funds and lets them DRIP into the sunset. They're just buying the funds their bosses tell them to. And if you are using a model, your advisor is definitely not calling the shots but getting paid as though she is.

In 50+ years of investing, I've almost never purchased less than 100 shares of anything. So if you see numbers other than 100, 200, 300, or fractional shares of your holdings, it's a sure sign your manager is taking DRIP investing shortcuts, using model portfolios, or both.

That's just not management, IMO.

In April 2023 when I retired, none of my clients were paying even 2 percent per year in fees. Their CEF portfolios were generating about four times that. As manager, my share was about one-third of the total fee charged. That gives you an idea what to expect if you decide to use a pro.

If you've got the time and courage, you can no doubt do better by yourself with this methodology than you would with any private manager who doesn't have CEF investing experience.

If the advisor brags about total return, doesn't know the income numbers for their approach, or uses "we think" recommendations, this is not the advisor for you. Your mission is to grow both working capital and realized base income. Not too many pros will even know what you're talking about.

If there is any doubt in your mind, go with a pro, at least for a short time, while you get comfortable with the process. I can help you make this kind of arrangement—and you just might like the convenience of having a CEF specialist handle your portfolios.

DO I FEEL READY TO BUILD MY OWN FUND UNIVERSES?

This is the key question when you're getting started. If you don't build well-screened universes following the QDI principles, you won't get great results. There are resources available—including my own CEF Facebook group—that can help with knowledge and support. Participants in The Income Coach Facebook Group are willing to share what they've learned. I sell customizable selection universe templates you can use to track prices, yields, and current distributions.

My experience helping investors manage their money is that it takes time to wean yourself from market value/total return thinking and embrace IFRI.

Here's a story from DIY investor Bill Hood, a 78-year-old ex-accountant who's invested in CEFs since 2015, using my selection universes.

> "I manage my CEF portfolio myself. I use CEF Connect for analysis before I make my CEF choices. I also belong to The Income Coach Facebook Group to review others' ideas.
>
> "I spend approximately 2-3 hours per market day making decisions and executing trades. I prefer making my own decisions and not paying an advisor, which would lower my ROI (return on investment) I make it a 'fun' job that I focus on daily.
>
> "My annualized distribution level is approximately 9 percent of working capital, which makes for a very comfortable lifestyle."

Maybe this story helps you see whether you'd find CEF investing a fun job yourself—or not.

HOW LONG WOULD IT TAKE ME TO BECOME KNOWLEDGEABLE ENOUGH TO DIY THIS?

Ultimately, many clients I've had in the past concluded they didn't want to put in scores of hours becoming a CEF investing expert. They delegated the whole thing to my former management firm and went off to enjoy life.

The old saying that "nobody cares more about your money than you do" is true. But an experienced CEF portfolio manager makes up for it with their depth of expertise. It can save you so much time—and could make you more money.

Here's a story from another Facebook-group member who decided to DIY it with some consulting help from me. Larry Loeffler is a 62-year-old retired cabinet maker living in Missouri.

> *"I'm a DIY investor mainly because of a small inheritance that included a Roth IRA through Charles Schwab.*
>
> *"I jumped in headfirst. I'd never invested in much of anything, and this opened my eyes to the enjoyment of buying and selling securities. Schwab's online trading platform is extremely user-friendly and updates multiple times per minute. Soon, I opened my own Roth and a regular brokerage account.*
>
> *"Granted, I made some stupid mistakes. But I also saved a lot in brokerage fees so that helped. With Steve's guidance and the CEF Facebook group, I can discuss various funds and how they relate to my portfolio.*
>
> *"Man, you can't pay for the kind of information these groups provide. That's one reason I nicknamed Steve our own personal Yoda." In April 2023, my distribution yield was over 10 percent.*

Reviewing these questions should give you a good feel for how you want to approach CEF investing: Totally DIY, DIY with help from a pro, or delegating the whole project to a professional investment manager.

DECISION TIME

It was time for the Cranes to decide how to invest in CEFs. I could see them quietly conferring with their audio muted. Then, they turned back to their camera.

"I almost feel like I've learned enough to DIY it," Jean said. "But I think being *able* to do it and wanting to spend a lot of my free time on it are two different things. I want to enjoy my leisure time more than I want to become a CEF investing expert.

"I think we're in the 'DIY with help' category," she concluded. John nodded.

"What if we work with your investing universes and get some consulting time with you?" he said. "I think we probably won't be watching every day for profit-taking opportunities. But we can make it work for us, if we don't have to do all the research on which CEFs to invest in."

Sounds great, I said. I'm happy to consult with you and walk you through using my selection universes.

"One other thing," she said. "I think my son-in-law and my daughter are more hands-on investors than we are. Could you talk to them, too? I think they might be DIYers, once they understand your approach."

You bet. First, let's set a time and place to meet and start helping you switch to income-focused retirement investing with CEFs. I'm excited to help you enjoy the rest of your retirement with a portfolio that produces more spending money than ever before.

It should be sometime before our Japan trip. I know you've started talking to Sandie about taking that together, I said, and I love the idea.

With your portfolio invested in CEFs, this time you should be able to cover the trip costs with your distribution income. No more selling securities and shrinking your working capital to pay your expenses, right?

"I definitely look forward to that," Jean said.

NEXT STEPS

Y OU MADE IT! Congrats on taking the time to learn a life-changing way to invest—not just for retirement but for your children and younger friends to use to reach financial independence sooner. Let's take a moment to step back and review all you've learned:

INCOME-FOCUSED RETIREMENT INVESTING IN A NUTSHELL

At this point, you've got the big picture. You've learned why traditional buy-and-hold investing rarely produces the level of income you'll need in retirement. I've demonstrated why closed-end funds are the best investing vehicle for generating retirement income from both stocks and bonds.

You learned to apply six principles for selecting and managing CEF portfolios:

1. Discover quality CEFs by using seven separate screening techniques.
2. Diversify based on financial risk, sector representation, growth or income focus, and position size.
3. Generate growing base income streams by using only securities paying more than 6 percent.
4. Take targeted profits dependent of where we are in the market cycle.
5. Use your understanding of the market cycles to fine-tune your investment decisions—both buying and selling—and to form valid performance expectations.
6. Assess investment performance only by focusing on base income and working-capital growth numbers.

Learning how to use these six principles was just the beginning. We talked through asset allocation and how to use the principles to fill your buckets with the best-quality growth- and income-purpose CEFs.

Next, you saw several IFRI examples. You also learned how to transition into CEF investing, either from a cash position or a traditional portfolio. You even learned how to switch only part of a traditional portfolio into CEFs.

You got a sense of the questions my Facebook-group investors ask, and you assessed whether you're more suited to DIY investing, hiring a pro to manage your portfolio, or managing your portfolio yourself with a little help from a consultant.

That last option is the role I fill these days—coaching self-managing investors of all ages on CEF investing.

You have a decision to make. Do you want to keep buying and holding, hoping and wishing that the markets don't crash? Or would you rather invest in a reliable system where you'll earn the income you need in retirement no matter what's happening in the markets?

If you'd like help investing in CEFs, here are some ways I can help.

FREE RESOURCES

In addition to the Resource Guide, I offer links to hundreds of investment articles—as well as links to a free webinar and several Q&A recordings—on my website, theincomecoach.net. The site also has information and pricing for my coaching services. And if you've gained some insights from what you've read here, please post a book review on Amazon, Goodreads, or in whatever social channels you use to tell your friends and family.

COACHING SERVICES

Want to work with me? I offer several levels of coaching:

- **BASIC ONE-ON-ONE OR FAMILY GROUP TELEPHONE/ZOOM MEETINGS** either involve a discussion of CEF investing, or I answer your questions and talk about goals and objectives. These run up to an hour and don't include much detailed portfolio review. These are fact-finding, goal-determining sessions to see if we can work well together to accomplish your goals.

- **PORTFOLIO REVIEW AND ACTION PLAN SESSIONS** include as many individual one-hour meetings as you need until you are where you want to be and ready to move forward on your own. All sessions are the same fee. Portfolios under $300,000 could be done in as few as two sessions, while larger portfolios may take several meetings to complete.
- **ADDITIONAL MEETINGS** for Q&As, more planning, or performance evaluation can be arranged. On-call, retainer fee arrangements can also be implemented.
- To book income coaching time with me, visit theincomecoach.net.

FACEBOOK GROUP: THE INCOME COACH

The Income Coach is a private Facebook support group for readers of *Retirement Money Secrets: A Financial Insider's Guide to Income Independence.* Anything about income investing as presented in the book is open for discussion in this group.

This group is for potential, current, and former coaching clients of mine. There are many experienced CEF investors to learn from in the group.

All my new articles and periodic selection universe reports are posted here. There are also periodic free Q&A Zoom meetings and occasional special discount offers. I hope to see you in the chat threads of the Facebook group.

SELECTION UNIVERSE SPREADSHEETS

The CEF Selection Universe spreadsheets I create to manage my own portfolios are available for purchase through The Retirement Income Coach website. They're updated monthly to provide distribution history and other analysis. They are included with any coaching purchase.

My selection universes typically contain 240 to 260 quality screened equity, taxable-income, and tax-free CEFs that meet my selection quality, income, and diversification standards.

PROFESSIONAL ADVISOR ASSIST ARRANGEMENTS

I work with insurance, healthcare, investment, real estate, accounting, and other professionals to bring Income Focused Retirement Investing information to their clients on a split-fee arrangement. Contact me for more information.

PROFESSIONAL INVESTMENT ADVISOR RETENTION ARRANGEMENTS

I can introduce you to investment advisors who specialize in IFRI investing and do individual portfolio management, just as I did in my former career. I receive a portion of their fee for making the introduction.

MODEL PORTFOLIO DISTRIBUTOR ARRANGEMENT

I've developed a set of model portfolios that implement the IFRI strategies. I'm seeking advisors, practices, or broker-dealers who might serve as the distributor in exchange for revenue participation. Contact me if you are interested.

GLOSSARY

Definitions of Investment Terms You Need to Understand

Investors need to be familiar with a lot of investment terminology. Here's a glossary of many of the terms in this book.

A

Analysis Paralysis: The tendency to overanalyze things. Analysis paralysis can make it difficult for investors to make timely decisions.

Annuity: An insurance-like product where the seller guarantees the return of your invested money, plus a small amount of interest in monthly installments until you die. Mostly return of capital.

Asset Allocation: The planning process for the division of investment portfolio assets between growth and income-purpose securities, based on the investor's personal financial situation, goals, and objectives.

ATH: An acronym for all-time high. During an ATH on any index, examine your portfolio for possible pruning decisions.

B

Base Income: The income derived from security dividends and interest, and CEF distributions alone, without including realized capital gains.

Book Value: The net value of a company's assets minus its liabilities.

Buy-and-Hold: The strategy of holding securities for the long term to watch market values increase and decrease over time.

C

Capital Gain: The profit from the sale of an asset. Profit-taking to capture capital gains can help grow investment income and working capital.

Capital Loss: When you sell an asset for less than your cost, you incur a capital loss.

CEF: An acronym for closed-end fund. A CEF is a professionally managed pass-through trust with a limited number of ownership shares. A CEF's shares trade like other equities. CEFs generally pay far more in distributions than either the securities they contain or mutual funds and ETFs containing the exact same securities. Most CEFs use leverage to increase income production.

Contractual Rate: The rate of interest a fixed-income security issuer pays to investors. A 4 percent bond, loan, T-bill, mortgage, or other fixed-income security pays fixed amounts of interest, and sometimes principal, on pre-set monthly, quarterly, or semi-annual dates until the maturity date. At maturity, the full face-value of the security is paid to the investor.

Correction: A period of generally falling prices in a market, identified by more securities moving lower in price than are moving higher for a significant period.

Cost Basis: The total amount invested in a security. The total cost basis of all portfolio securities plus cash equals total working capital.

D

Day-Limit Order: An order to purchase a security at a specific price. It expires at the end of that trading day.

Debt Securities: Negotiable securities issued by municipalities, corporations, governments, and others, which are contractual obligations to pay periodic interest at a specific rate and the total principal at maturity.

Discount/Premium: Debt securities trade at a discount to par value (see below) when prevailing interest rates are above their own contractual rate and at a premium when prevailing rates are below that rate. At maturity, the par value of each security is repaid.

Diversification: One of the big four portfolio financial-risk minimizers, diversification is a management technique that keeps the cost basis of each security well below 5 percent of the total portfolio. Diversification should be considered in many other ways too: for instance, by geography, industry, financial risk, management firm, and position size.

Dollar-Cost Averaging: The strategy of regularly investing in a security no matter what its current market price. The result is generally a higher cost basis and lower yield, as some investments will occur at inopportune times.

DRIP: An acronym for Dividend Reinvestment Plan. DRIPs are a form of dollar-cost averaging in which base income from a security is automatically reinvested back into that same security. Over time, dripping makes portfolios less diverse and leads to a higher cost basis and lower yield.

E

Equity Securities: Equity securities (common stocks) represent an ownership interest in the issuing company. Equities are riskier than debt securities, as interest on debt must be paid before any shareholder payouts, even in bankruptcy.

Equity Bucket: The asset allocation location of all portfolio equity securities and uninvested cash. CEFs containing more than 35 percent equities are included.

ETF: An acronym for exchange traded fund. These funds trade like stocks and usually track a particular index, sector, or other collection of securities. They are essentially unmanaged, although a managed variety is developing. Like mutual funds, their prices are manipulated to equalize share price with the NAV.

F

Fixed-Income Securities: Securities that pay a regular recurring, specific amount of interest or dividend income. All bonds and preferred stocks are deemed fixed-income securities.

Float: The total number of outstanding shares of an individual company or CEF. ETFs and mutual funds have an unlimited number of shares.

GHI

Growth Bucket: In asset allocation, the set of securities chosen primarily for profit-taking opportunities. Any fund or CEF containing more than 35 percent equities would be included.

Income: One of the four risk minimizers, income is what a security pays to owners in the form of interest, dividends, or other payouts.

Income Bucket: In asset allocation, securities whose primary purpose is to generate regular income. Any fund containing at least 65 percent income-purpose securities would be included.

IFRI: An acronym for Income-Focused Retirement Investing, which is the CEF investing system I've taught you in this book. The goal of IFRI is to construct a portfolio that generates enough income to more than pay your bills, regardless of what's happening in the markets and without dipping into principal.

Inflation: A measure of reduced purchasing power due to higher prices. Only rising income can keep pace with inflation.

IRE: An acronym for interest-rate expectations—the buzz in the investment community about where interest rates are headed. More than actual interest-rate changes, IRE tends to influence markets.

Invasion of Principal: When you need to withdraw more from your portfolio than the income it generates, you must sell some securities to get more money. This is known as invasion of principal. You're liquidating some of your working capital, which lowers base income in the future.

Investment Portfolio: The securities and other marketable assets that you consider to be investments, as opposed to things like homes, cars, furniture, and jewelry, which are usually not investment property. Your portfolio may contain all manner of investment vehicles.

IPO: An acronym for initial public offering. An IPO can be for an individual security or a fund. The price includes all the marketing costs of the issue. Generally speaking, IPOs are highly speculative investments that rarely pay income. CEFs are an exception as they typically start to pay distributions much sooner. I don't invest in any CEFs less than five years in operation.

JKL

Leverage: A strategy that involves borrowing money at X percent and investing it at X+ percent to increase either profits or investment income. This strategy is used regularly by CEF managers and by almost every other business entity.

Liquidity: A measure of the ability to buy or sell a security immediately. Liquidity is mostly affected by float.

Market and Interest Rate Cycles: The up-and-down movement of interest rates and market indices, often measured from one peak or trough to the next, with no less than a year between the two.

MCIM: An acronym for market-cycle investment management, a management style I developed in the 1970s to take advantage of market movements.

Market Order: A buy or sell order that means you are willing to accept the next price offered or bid for the security you are buying or selling. Market orders should never be used.

Market Risk: The perceived risk that an investor will lose money due to broad downward market movements. For the IFRI investor, downward market movements are opportunities. Market risk is a known feature of all securities and is more of a certainty than a risk.

Market Timing: Investing based on predictions of where markets are headed, in an attempt to buy low or sell high. However, regular successful marketing timing is impossible.

Market Value: The amount buyers would be willing to pay for the securities in your portfolio at any point. You can't spend market value.

Master Limited Partnerships: A publicly traded business venture structure that's industry focused and as such, more risky than diversified investments.

Mutual Fund: A fund that pools investor money and invests it in securities. Mutual funds' unlimited number of common shares represent ownership of an indeterminable fraction of the securities held within the fund. They are not tradable during the market day, and buy/sell decisions are not totally at the discretion of the manager.

N

NAV: An acronym for net asset value. The NAV of an ETF, mutual fund, or CEF is the difference between its assets and liabilities, like the book value of a corporate entity. Neither stock nor CEF prices are directly related to the NAV. The NAV of a CEF reflects the current market price of hundreds of securities, while CEF prices reflect supply and demand and are not tied to the NAV.

O

Opportunity Cost or Risk: The amount of potential gain an investor misses out on when they commit to one investment choice over another. Purely hypothetical or the product of hindsight.

P

Par Value: The face value of a debt security or a preferred stock. Typically, what the investor receives at maturity.

Peak-to-Peak Analysis: Analyzing portfolio market value performance in a period defined by two peaks in a market index, separated by at least 12 months. It's a much more meaningful way of assessing performance than a calendar-year comparison.

Position Size: Investors refer to their individual security holdings as positions. The size of each position in a portfolio is used as a diversification test. No position should ever approach 5 percent of the portfolio. This test is always based on working capital, not market value.

Principal: The amount invested in a security or securities. Also, the amount of the remaining debt owed on a loan.

Profit-Taking: One of the four great portfolio risk minimizers, profit-taking involves selling a security at a profit to generate cash to either reinvest or to spend. When reinvested, it accelerates growth in both income and working capital.

Pruning: The practice of selling off portions of a portfolio's poorest-performing securities, using individual purchase or tax lots.

Q

QDI + PT: An acronym for Quality, Diversification, Income and Profit-Taking, the four great financial-risk minimizers.

Quality: One of the four risk minimizers, quality assesses such factors as a fund's or security's age and distribution history, diversification, and income production. The most important of all the risk minimizers.

R

REIT: An acronym for real estate investment trust. A publicly traded REIT is similar to a CEF and purchased primarily as an income security. *Private REITs are illiquid, dangerous, speculative, and to be avoided.*

ROC: An acronym for return of capital. Part of the distribution from some CEFs, ROC could consist of anything from mortgage principal to premiums on option trades. An ROC payout results in a dollar-for-dollar reduction in the cost basis of the paying security. ROC is only destructive if spent.

Rights Offerings: A method used by companies and CEFs to expand their float by bringing new shares to the market. Existing owners have the right to buy shares based on their existing holdings to avoid dilution of their interest in the company or CEF. I treat them as I do special distributions—free extra money to selectively reinvest.

S

Selection Universe: The hundreds of CEFs that meet our QDI-based selection criteria.

Sell Target: The point at which you plan to sell a security. The sell target will vary based on the number of quality available replacement CEFs. It can be as low as "any profit" during corrections and as high as 5 percent during rallies.

Spread: The spread is the difference between the "bid" price (what the buyer is willing to pay) and the "asked" price (what the seller is willing to accept). CEF spreads are larger than those of most stocks and ETFs.

T

Tax-Exempt Securities: Interest on municipal bonds is exempt from federal income tax but taxed by all but the state of origin. Check with your accountant to see if a tax-free investment makes sense for you.

Tax Lots: When a security position is developed over time, each individual purchase is monitored as a separate "lot" for tax purposes, even in non-taxable portfolios. Tax-lot trimming can create realized profits in pieces of positions and is an income and capital acceleration strategy best used in the early stages of rallies. Make sure your investment platform allows you to trade lots selectively in your qualified plan accounts.

Total Return: A measure of your portfolio's market value gain or loss in a calendar year. Since market value can't be spent, this figure represents only paper gains or losses.

Total Realized Return: The net amount of base income and capital gains produced by your portfolio in a given period, usually a year. *Total realized return* is money you can spend or reinvest.

UV

Variable Income Security: A security that pays different amounts over time, by design. Examples include royalty trusts, REITs, unit trusts, and Government National Mortgage Association unit trusts. Some CEFs pay variable distributions.

Velocity of Money: The rate at which new working capital is created by profit-taking and reinvestment of income distributions. More frequent profits mean stronger growth in both working capital and distribution income.

W

Working Capital: The total cost basis of the securities and cash in your portfolio.

XYZ

Z-Score: A Z-score represents the distance of a CEF's price premium or discount from its average premium or discount for a particular time frame. This is used by some as an indication of how expensive or cheap a CEF is relative to its own price history. Personally, I don't use them.

ACKNOWLEDGEMENTS

THIS BOOK WOULDN'T exist without the earliest partners in developing my Income-Focused Retirement Investing approach: the hundreds of clients I've worked with over the years. Two I must mention by name—my close friends Domenico Belcastro (the owner of Domenico's Restaurant in Levittown, New York) and Dr. Winfred Ginter, DDS, of Lake Hopatcong, New Jersey. They were my first clients in 1979 and were still with me when I retired from investment management in 2023.

I must also thank four members of various CEF Facebook groups who worked with me to develop *Retirement Money Secrets*. Will Allender, Bryan Finnegan, Scott Phillips, and Craig Goldstein spent many hours and sat through many meetings to help get the book from outline to final manuscript.

Many other members of the Facebook CEF groups also played important roles. They encouraged the effort and participated in many Q&As that developed book content. You heard from Bill Hood, Larry Laufler, and Robin Fleetwood as they generously contributed their personal experiences. David Fleming and George Cain also participated.

Also important to the book's creation was Seattle-based ghostwriter extraordinaire Carol Tice, a well-known and widely published business journalist, book author, and digital-business entrepreneur. She came up with the book's conversational structure, which helped me explain concepts in layman's terms and avoid financial jargon that might put off newcomers to CEF investing. Carol has ghosted many books and written more than a dozen books and e-books under her own byline. I highly recommend her—find her at caroltice.com.

Through Carol, I connected with two other professionals who made great contributions to the book, Marla Markman of Markman Editorial Services (www.marlamarkman.com). and book design/publication superstar Caerus Kourt of Bookery.

Saving the most important for last, there's my wife Sandie. For the second time, she's put up with my compulsive— nearly all-consuming dedication of time and resources to a book project. She patiently helped, proofed, cautioned, edited, and reality checked the manuscript. I'm confident she was thrilled when publication was finalized, and our new semi-retirement life could begin.

Made in United States
Orlando, FL
02 April 2024